Why can't computer books be easier to understand?

Not all of us want to become computer professionals, but we do want to have fun with our computers and be productive. The new *Simple Guides* cover the popular topics in computing. Most importantly, they are simple to understand. Each book in the series introduces the main features of a topic and shows you how to get the most from your PC.

Simple Guides – No gimmicks, no jargon, no fuss

Available in the *Simple Guides* series:

The Internet	Web design
Searching the Interenet	Using spreadsheets
The PC	Using email
Office 2000	Putting audio and video on your website
Windows 98	Writing for your website
E-commerce	Dreamweaver 4
Digital cameras, scanning and using images	Flash 5 for Windows

A simple guide to

internet research

Greg Spence

Prentice
Hall

An imprint of PEARSON EDUCATION

Pearson Education Limited

Head Office:
Edinburgh Gate
Harlow
Essex CM20 2JE
Tel: +44 (0)1279 623623
Fax: +44 (0)1279 431059

London Office:
128 Long Acre
London WC2E 9AN
Tel: +44 (0)20 7447 2000
Fax: +44 (0)20 7240 5771
website: www.informit.uk.com

First published in Great Britain 2001
© Pearson Education Limited 2001

ISBN 0-130-60865-3

The right of Greg Spence to be identified as the author of this work has been asserted by him in accordance with the Copyright, Designs and Patents Act 1988.

British Library Cataloguing in Publication Data
A CIP catalogue record for this book can be obtained from the British Library.

10 9 8 7 6 5 4 3 2 1

Typeset by Pantek Arts Ltd, Maidstone, Kent
Printed and bound in Great Britain by Ashford Colour Press, Gosport, Hampshire.

The publishers' policy is to use paper manufactured from sustainable forests.

Contents

6 Other internet tools 97

Acknowledgements

A book is produced not just by its author but by a great many people who work in the background. I would like to thank Clare Christian, Editor of the Simple Guide series, for having the faith in my manuscript to see it through to publication. Thank you Clare, and congratulations on the birth of your baby during the production of this book!

I would also like to thank Steve Temblett, Senior Acquisitions Editor, who has now worked with me on two books. Steve continues to have faith in my writing and I appreciate his ongoing support and encouragement.

I would also like to thank the production team at Pearson Education for taking my manuscript, correcting it where required, and getting this book onto the bookshelves. Thanks all.

Finally I would like to thank my long-suffering family who have stood by me during many long hours of typing. Thank you to my wife Katrina, my daughter Katherine, and my son Alex.

Any errors or omissions are entirely down to me, although I cannot be held responsible for any websites I may have quoted which no longer exist (they were available at the time of publication). Websites come and go and no book can take account of that. That is the nature of the internet.

Greg Spence

Southampton, Hants, UK.

Introduction

On the internet you can access millions of web pages, documents, images and sounds covering thousands of topics. The problem is finding high-quality information quickly, easily and with a minimum amount of time online.

Learning to intelligently use search tools, many of which are available to you for free, can be time consuming, as can searching for that resource that you know is out there somewhere in cyberspace if only you could get to it!

The internet, with its vast array of resources, promises to be a goldmine for a researcher who is trying to further her knowledge of a specific subject. The problem is knowing where to start and how to refine your search so that you find only the web pages and documents of direct relevance to you, thereby avoiding information overload.

Congratulations on finding this guide. You are about to learn how to become a more proficient internet searcher.

How do I use this book?

The book is divided into 12 chapters as follows:

- Chapter 1 discusses why the internet can be a useful source of research. The pros and cons are also discussed, together with the common mistakes beginners make while searching online.

- Chapter 2 introduces some terms that you will encounter as you begin to search the vastness of cyberspace. I will also introduce the importance of planning what you want to find before you begin, to help you save time.
- Chapter 3 introduces you to the basic search tools available on the internet and shows you how to decide which type of search tool to use depending on the sort of information you are looking for.
- Chapter 4 discusses the capabilities of the search engines and directories you are likely to use for your research. This chapter also covers how they are used and describes a number of search techniques you can use to get the most out of each tool. You will also learn how to locate those harder-to-find resources that the search engines and directories are not able to index. This part of the internet is known as the 'invisible web'.
- Chapter 5 shows you how email can be used as a search tool. If you do not have access to the World Wide Web (WWW) or a web browser, this chapter will be of interest to you as it shows you how to get information by email alone.
- Chapter 6 discusses other tools that allow you to access more specialised information. If you are looking for people or for a specific email address, want to keep abreast of the latest news or need to access reference information, then this chapter is for you.
- Chapter 7 covers how to automate your searches using software 'bots' that will notify you when something of interest to you appears on the internet.
- Chapter 8 discusses each of the different file types you are likely to encounter, shows you how to save the results of your searches, and how to download data in a format that can be loaded into a spreadsheet or database program. You will learn how to best organise your search results so you can find them again.

- Chapter 9 covers some of the commercially available software programs that can help you to perform your research faster and deeper.

- Chapter 10 explains that not all documents, articles and reports you will find online will be accurate or authoritative. In this chapter you will discover a technique you can use to help you quickly evaluate both the usefulness of a document or web page and its accuracy.

- Chapter 11 contains a case study that illustrates how to use the techniques described in this guide when researching your family tree. The principles taught in this case study can be used for any type of research.

- Chapter 12 takes a glimpse into the future of search technologies.

- The Appendices contain a full list of internet domain name extensions listed by country. So if you want to know the extension used by sites registered in Germany, for example (which is '.de' by the way), you can find it here. I have also included some worksheets you can use when planning your searches and evaluating resources. The use of these worksheets is covered in Chapters 2 and 10.

Conventions and icons

Throughout the book notes have been included, each of which is associated with an icon:

Provides additional information about the subject concerned.

Indicates a variety of shortcuts: keyboard shortcuts, 'Wizard' options, techniques reserved for experts, etc.

Warns you of the risks associated with a particular action and, where necessary, shows you how to avoid any pitfalls.

Why use the internet for research?

The pros and cons of the internet as a research tool

The common mistakes beginners make

1

Before we learn how to use the internet to research our specialist subject, it would be useful to understand why the internet can be used for this purpose, the pros and cons of using it, and the common mistakes newcomers to the internet often make when searching for information.

The biggest attraction of the internet to researchers, writers, journalists, newsletter editors, teachers and educationalists is the potential to tap into millions of documents, reports, websites, research papers, images and sounds that are held on thousands of computer systems worldwide.

Until around 15 years ago the internet was still largely used only by educational institutions for passing research information around various college campuses. This led to the storage of a large amount of statistical data, research reports, and documents of immediate interest to educationalists and teachers. As the internet spread to the outside world of commercial organisations and private consumers began to access what became the World Wide Web, the nature of this information changed and grew.

Today it is possible to obtain information on any subject, from nuclear fusion to methods of getting rid of moles from your garden. This vast store of data is accessible from anywhere in the world to anyone who wants it and knows how to get it. Granted, some data may be sensitive and therefore only accessible with a username and password, while other types of information are commercial and can be accessed only by way of a subscription fee.

The biggest problem is that due to the vastness of the internet, someone searching for information on, for example, healthcare can end up being confronted with thousands of websites devoted to the subject! Herein lies the problem. It is very easy to suffer from data overload and as a result a failure to assemble the data into meaningful information. This is where this guide is designed to help.

By learning a series of simple search techniques it will be possible for you to quickly home in on the information you seek. What's more, the resources you find will be directly relevant to the subject in hand. By combining these simple techniques with the power of the search engines it is possible to be productive on the internet in a very short space of time.

The pros and cons of the internet as a research tool

To use the internet effectively you need to know what it can and cannot deliver. The internet can be very frustrating, the quality of the information you find on it is variable, it is not fully indexed, and it is far from comprehensive. So you may ask, is it worth using it at all as a research aid? My answer to that question is a definite yes!

Using the internet, you will be able to find data not available anywhere else. It is especially useful for locating out-of-print books and reports that will still be useful to you. And with the phenomenal acceptance of the internet as a medium for the transfer of knowledge, more and more people are publishing their work on the internet alone.

However, just because you have discovered the internet does not mean that you will no longer find the library of any use to you. In fact, not only will you be able to use your local library's reference facilities more effectively, you will also be able to make use of libraries around the world as many of them now have their own websites.

The Internet, sometimes called simply 'the Net,' is a worldwide system of computer networks – a network of networks in which users at any one computer can, if they have permission, get information from any other computer. The world wide web (WWW) consists of all the resources and users on the Internet that are using the Hypertext Transfer Protocol (HTTP). Typically any web page which is linked to another on a different web site forms part of the world wide web. HTTP is the set of rules for exchanging files (text, graphic images, sound, video, and other multimedia files) on the world wide web.

One major advantage of using a computer as a search vehicle is that when you find a report or document of interest it can be downloaded to your computer and is already in a form that can be used in a word processor. Photocopying information from a library reference book still requires you to type it into your word processor!

When searching, you need to be realistic and focused about what you want to find. Do you want a precise fact, a specific report, or more general background material? You also need to be disciplined. You need to know when to stop.

How will you know when you have enough information, when do you decide the data you want is just not available? I cannot provide you with answers to these questions as the answers can come only with experience. What I can show you though is how to quickly find information that is directly relevant to your needs which avoids you wandering aimlessly around the cyberjungle.

The common mistakes beginners make

When you are new to the internet it can be a very intimidating place. Not only are you faced with the task of knowing where to start your search, but you also need to know *how* to search.

The first thing a beginner will do is use one of the major search engines such as AltaVista or Excite, and directories such as Yahoo!. This is because these tools are cited as being the most popular mechanism for finding information. The beginner will then enter a vague search word such as 'music' and end up with a list of millions of websites to visit.

It is true that search engines will form a large part of your 'surfing' life on the internet, but they are not the only tools available to you and nor should they be. In fact, there are millions of documents that are still not accessible via the well-known search engines and directories on the World Wide Web but are available on the internet.

What is the difference between the WWW and the internet? You probably thought they were the same thing. This is a common misconception.

When the internet started it was simply a network of computers, each of which contained many files. Some were text files, others were software programs, while others were files stored in binary which needed to be converted before they could be read by a human. These files were accessed using software that could only be operated by computer technicians. Depending on the file they accessed, they might have had to convert it to a human-readable form before the file could be used. The computer technician would understand whether or not a file needed conversion simply by looking at its name, or by looking inside it.

For the internet to gain wider acceptance, some means of storing and retrieving data so that anyone could find it and read it, without having to have a degree in computer science, had to be developed. Enter Tim Berners-Lee and the CERN research laboratory.

While Tim was working at CERN in Switzerland he developed the language called HTML, which stands for Hypertext Markup Language. This language allows codes to be hidden within text documents so that they can be displayed on a computer screen. Together with the language, a means of reading HTML documents and interpreting them had to be developed – enter the web browser.

The most common two web browsers are Netscape Navigator from Netscape and Internet Explorer from Microsoft.

These two components made it possible for web pages to be developed and for them to be viewed by anyone who has access to a suitable browser and knows how to use it.

HTML also allows documents to be linked to each other by way of a web address known as a URL, or Uniform Resource Locator. The URL may point to another machine, in a different country, containing a document of interest to you. When you click on the URL, the web browser sends a command to that machine to get the document and display it for you. As a user of the browser you do not have to be concerned about which machine the document resides on, or how to access it. All of that is handled for you behind the scenes.

However, not all documents can be accessed this way because there are many millions that have yet to be hyperlinked (as it is called) on HTML web pages. The good news is we can still get to these documents using nothing other than an email program. In Chapter 5 I will show you how to do this.

The other important fact you must know is how to use the search engines and other research tools so that they return only websites and documents of direct relevance to the search you are conducting.

As I mentioned earlier, it is very easy to enter a word, ask the search engine to find all web pages containing that word, and for the engine to return thousands of websites that may or may not be of the slightest interest. It is possible to tell the search engines exactly what you are looking for by using special

Now that you know that the WWW and the internet are not the same, you will understand the importance of having to use more than one tool when conducting research.

syntax. The problem is that each search engine uses a slightly different syntax to achieve this. We will be looking at what syntax the major search engines have in common, and how they differ, so that you can make more intelligent and effective searches of the WWW.

When you combine this knowledge with the search techniques that I will teach you, you will rapidly become a power searcher and be able to find any document you want with ease.

A search strategy

First, learn the language

Plan the road ahead

First, learn the language

During your searching you may come across several terms associated with the internet and the WWW with which you are probably not familiar. Let's take a quick look at the most common ones before we go any further.

Domain – the last part of an internet address which indicates either the type of website, the country where the website is based, or both. For example '.com' indicates a commercial internet site, '.mil' a military internet site, '.net' internet network gateways, '.uk' a UK-based site, '.it' an Italian site (for a full list see Appendix A).

Domain name, URL, website address – these terms all refer to the address of a website. For example, the website address (or domain name or URL) for the publisher of this guide is **http://www.pearson.com**. In Chapter 10 I will explain what each part of a URL stands for.

Host – the computer where a web page is located.

Meta search – a search that queries several different resources at the same time. For example, a meta search engine (discussed in Chapter 4) will query several different general search engines at the same time from a single search request.

Wildcard – a symbol used to denote a number of missing letters in a search word or phrase, usually a '*'.

Spider – a software program which indexes a website by following all the hyperlinks it finds on each page. This is the mechanism used by a search engine to populate and update its index.

Bot – a software program that performs some job automatically. For example, a search bot can find websites of interest and email the URLs to you.

Hyperlink – text that is highlighted on a web page and when clicked on will take you to another website, another page on the same website, a document, image, sound file or video clip.

Dead link – a hyperlink that no longer works because the resource it points to is no longer available.

Search engine – a software program that will locate a website or other resource by searching an index.

Directory – an index of websites and other resources compiled and maintained by human beings instead of a spider.

HTML – stands for Hypertext Markup Language, the commands used to create a web page.

http – stands for Hypertext Transfer Protocol, the mechanism used to get and display a web page in a browser.

Web browser – a software program installed on your computer that enables you to display web pages. The most common web browsers are Netscape Navigator and Internet Explorer.

Usenet newsgroup, forum – a discussion list where people come together to discuss a specific subject.

Mailing list – similar to a usenet newsgroup or forum but each message is sent to the discussion group participants via email.

Keyword – a single word used in a search engine to find resources.

Search phrase – two or more words used in a search engine to find resources.

Portal – a website that links to several resources covering a specific subject.

Results page – a list of resources found by a search engine in response to a keyword or search phrase.

Plan the road ahead

If you are not careful your time online can be frittered away and before you know it you will have been online for five hours and still not found entirely what you are looking for. Have you ever been in that position? I know I have and it is not a pleasant feeling to know that somewhere in cyberspace is the information you so desperately need if only you could get to it.

'Surfing the internet' is a phrase frequently used to refer to searching and visiting websites one by one in the vain hope of finding something of use. You may have read about the fact that website visitors are impatient people who will spend only a maximum of 30 seconds on a website before they have to move on. Very often this is because they may have arrived at a site thinking it is going to give them the knowledge they were seeking, only to find out it doesn't.

Going through a list of websites in the vain hope that they might provide you with valuable data is not the most intelligent way of spending your time online. What we need is a strategy that will get us to where we want to be more quickly, so we can spend longer on those websites that *do* match our requirements.

Before you go online you should sit down and think about exactly what you are hoping to get out of your time on the internet. Follow this strategy and you should be able to get this information in a matter of minutes.

A search strategy

If you are new to the internet it would make sense to follow this strategy to the letter. Once you become familiar with what works and what doesn't you may devise your own strategy for searching.

Before you go online it is imperative that you plan your research. By planning you will avoid spending hours perusing websites that contribute nothing to furthering your knowledge and you will make more efficient use of the time you are online.

Before you start:

- Determine exactly what you are searching for (statistics, background information, sources, information about a particular person).
- Decide whether you are trying to confirm a fact, find new information for the first time or add to your knowledge of a subject.
- Work out what type of resources would be most useful to you (reports, articles, government records).
- Write down the name of any leading experts in your subject area. Can you consult them via email? Do they have a website?
- Determine whether the information you are seeking is likely to be available online. If it is confidential, you may not be able to find it.
- Decide which search tool is most appropriate to your needs.
- Make sure you understand how to use the advanced search capabilities of the tool.

Addressing each of these points will give you a framework within which you can begin to frame your search requirements and which you can use to keep you on track during your searching.

Do not always use your favourite search engine, it may not be appropriate for every search. Do not assume that all the results that are returned are directly relevant to your query.

To help you I have included in Appendix B a search strategy worksheet. Use it to make a record of your search plan and to record your progress.

Choose your search phrases carefully

A large percentage of your success will depend on the search phrases you choose. Very often the importance of choosing a relevant search phrase is overlooked. A good rule of thumb here is to choose words that can quickly narrow down your search. Select words that are unique or peculiar to your subject.

You also need to understand that different search engines accomplish their job by taking different approaches to indexing the web. Some engines index every word of every page, some index the first 100 words, some index every word and filter out prepositions, conjunctions and common verbs. These common words include 'and, about, of, why, never, before, it, to, a, but, the, are, is, at, be, not, or'.

For example, let's assume I want to find the origin of the well known phrase 'to be or not to be'. If I enter this as a search phrase at the Excite search engine, Excite will report that there are no results to return! The reason for this is that the phrase contains nothing but common words, which Excite does not index. If I enter the same phrase at AltaVista it will return a large number of results, many of which are irrelevant. However, AltaVista does suggest an alternative search phrase to use. This can be seen in Figure 2.1 where AltaVista has suggested I use the phrase 'hamlet to be or not to be'. Very useful.

The next potential pitfall you should be aware of when choosing appropriate words and phrases for your search is cultural differences across the world. Words that are commonly used in the UK may be either spelled differently or have a different meaning elsewhere. You should also allow for common misspellings of words as they can very often return search results not found with the correct spelling.

You should use mainly nouns in your search phrase.

Figure 2.1 AltaVista will suggest an alternative search phrase if your initial search phrase is not specific enough.

There are many words that are often ignored by search engines because of their common use on the internet. Words such as 'computer, internet, software, web' may be ignored if they appear in your search phrase. If you want them to always be used, enclose them within quotes in your search, eg "internet software".

Finally, search engines are easily confused by heteronyms, which are words that have different meanings when pronounced differently. For example 'lead' (pronounced led), as in the metal, and 'lead' (pronounced leed). Make sure you either avoid these or make your meaning clear within the context of your search phrase.

Use advanced search techniques

Most search engines have the ability to perform either a simple or an advanced search. An advanced search allows you to enter complex phrases to narrow down your searches and hopefully make the search results more relevant.

I would recommend always using the advanced search, which will involve you having to come to terms with boolean logic. Now before you run into a dark corner, let me tell you that boolean logic is very simple to learn: it involves using the words 'NOT, AND, OR' in combination with your search phrase.

Unfortunately for us each search engine treats boolean logic slightly differently. I will explain the subtle differences and how you can get around them in Chapter 4.

Another technique worth using is 'field searching'. This gives you the ability to specify which fields the search engine should look in for your search phrase. For example, you can tell a search engine to check only each website URL for a match, or the title of the web page. You can even limit your search to a specific website. To do this you would enter a special keyword in front of your search phrase.

Let's say we wanted to search for 'family tree' and we only wanted web pages that had this phrase in their title to be returned on the results page. To achieve this we would enter

`title: "family tree"`

in the search box.

To limit my search to within a single website I would enter

`site:www.familysearch.org "family tree"`

which would look for the phrase 'family tree' only on the family search website.

Execute your search step by step
The art of successful searching is to be methodical. Follow the steps outlined above to plan your research activity, then execute it as follows (use the search strategy checklist in Appendix B to record what you are going to do):

- Can any particular company, association, or specialist organisation hold the information you need? Very often you may need to visit only one site to find what you need, especially if that site is dedicated to your search topic. Before trying the larger directories and search engines, try to guess the website address of the company, association or organisation. Start with **www.name-ofcompany.com**. If it is a government site, then **www.nameofagency.gov**

Notice I have put the phrase 'family tree' in quotes. This forces most search engines to only find web pages that match this phrase exactly. See Chapter 4 for more details on using this syntax. If I wanted to find this phrase in a website address I would enter url:"family tree".

may get you there. If it is a defence establishment, '.mil' will be useful. In other countries you will need to also use '.co.uk' for the UK, '.de' for Germany, etc. See Appendix A for a full list of URL extensions by country and type of domain.

■ If you have found a site that sort of covers what you want but does not satisfy you totally, check to see who is linking to the site you have found. Go to **http://www.altavista.com** and enter in the search box **link:nameof site.com** (or .gov, or .mil, etc). This will give you a list of similar sites you can now visit. Of course, you can use this method to also find out who is linking to them and so on. Another site that is useful for this is LinkPopularity, which can be found at **http://www.linkpopularity.com**. This will search multiple search engines for links to the website you entered.

■ If you were not able to guess the name of a suitable site, go to a directory such as Yahoo! (**http://www.yahoo.com**) and browse by your subject category. Visit the sites listed there but also make a note of the sub-categories you selected to get to them. They can be used as keywords in the search engines to find even more sites.

■ If you are looking for product information, use a specialised subject directory instead of a general directory (see Chapter 4).

■ Go to Ask Jeeves at **http://www.ask.com** (or **http://www.ask.co.uk**) and enter your search as a question, such as 'Where can I find sites on genealogy?'. This will return a mixture of websites, subject directories and other resources you can explore.

■ If you still have not found what you are looking for, then enter your search keywords (written down from your directory browsing) in the major search engines. **Do not enter single words** in the search box. You will get too many websites and become overwhelmed. Instead **enter a search phrase**. For example, instead of entering 'genealogy' which would return thousands of sites, enter 'genealogy uk' instead. Try to make your search phrase as narrow as possible. If you do not get any sites returned, then broaden your search slightly until you do.

Finding information

Introducing the tools of the trade

The right tools for the job

Introducing the tools of the trade

In order to be able to find the information you are seeking you need to know what tools are available, where you can find them, and more importantly how to use them effectively. In this chapter I will introduce you to these tools and show you a simple way to decide which tool to use when. In the next chapter I will show you how to use them.

The growth rate of the internet is nothing short of phenomenal. Hundreds of thousands of websites are appearing every month on every subject under the sun. Needless to say it is impossible for any one search engine, directory, or research tool to be able to index the entire web. In fact it is commonly quoted that no more than 40% of all websites are indexed in the search engines and directories.

For this reason no one search engine or directory will be able to find all the sources you may need, so you should be prepared to always use more than one tool during your searching. Which tool you use will depend on the subject you are researching and the type of information you require.

The two most commonly used tools are search engines and directories. If you are new to the net, or consider yourself a beginner, then you should focus your efforts on getting to know these two types of tools.

Once you become more proficient, or if you need to expand your search, then you should get to know the meta search engines. These types of tools use multiple search engines to find the data you want. In other words, a search engine which uses other search engines to do its job!

Still with me so far?

Taking this another step further you may want to get to know the many and varied subject directories that are popping up all over the place. These are directories dedicated to a specific topic, or series of related topics, which act as a one-stop source of information. I will discuss these in more detail in the next chapter.

Finally, there is one 'search engine' that is commonly overlooked, or not even considered to be able to perform searches. This is your email program.

Yes, I know what you are thinking, how can an email program search the internet? In Chapter 5 I will answer that question for you.

For now let's just say that if you do not have access to a web browser (and there are still lots of people who don't), or you cannot afford the expensive telephone charges you are running up whilst performing your searches (especially if you live in Europe like I do!), then email can be a very cost effective way of finding information. In fact email can search directories like Yahoo! and interrogate search engines like AltaVista – but more of that later.

Search engines
A search engine is simply a database containing thousands of links to websites. There are over 2500 search engines available and they all vary according to the types of websites they index, the amount of coverage of the web that they say they have, the features they have for searching, and their speed of operation.

The good news is that you do not need to use anywhere near 2500 engines to find what you need. In fact you will find yourself using at most five or six of the bigger engines. These will include AltaVista at **http://www.altavista.com** (or

http://www.altavista.co.uk), Excite at **http://www.excite.com**, Northern Light at **http://www.northernlight.com**, Hotbot at **http://www.hotbot.com**, Go at **http://www.go.com** and Google at **http://www.google.com**.

One thing that all search engines have in common is that if you use the same search keywords they will all return different results. Some will be more complete than others. The reason for this is that they have different ways of indexing websites.

Some engines use robots (also known as spiders) to discover websites. A robot, or spider, is simply a piece of computer software that goes out looking for new sites, or checks to see if sites that are already indexed still exist. Other engines rely on webmasters to submit their website to them for inclusion in their listings.

The other difference between the search engines is *how* they search their database of links. For example, if you were to search for 'rock music', one engine may return all websites that contain the word 'rock' and the word 'music'. Therefore you may get sites that talk about the rock formations in the Canadian Rockies together with other sites that cover all types of music from jazz to classical. The chances are there may be some sites that cover what you were really looking for which is 'rock music'!

If you were to perform the same search in other engines they may first search for all sites containing the word 'rock' and then from this list look for all the sites that contain the word 'music' and just return those. That would certainly give us a smaller, and perhaps more focused, list.

So you see it is important to know not only what you are looking for, but how to phrase it depending on the search engine you are using. It is this fact that makes searching the internet a real challenge.

Directories

A directory differs from a search engine due to the fact that it does not simply consist of a long list of links. A directory takes this one stage further by grouping the links into meaningful categories.

To use our 'rock music' example again. If I were to go to a directory I could click on a subject category of, say, Arts and Entertainment, which would then give me a list of sub-categories. From this list I would choose Music, which would then probably give me another list of sub-categories, one of which may be Rock.

The fundamental difference here is that I did not enter any keywords; I simply kept choosing from a category until I got to where I wanted to be. Yahoo! is perhaps the most famous example of this type of directory although it does also have the ability to search by keyword as well.

Typically directories are populated by human beings rather than software robots. Yahoo! (**http://www.yahoo.com** or **http://www.yahoo.co.uk**) is built this way. Many people review websites, decide if they are of sufficient quality for inclusion in the Yahoo! directory, and then categorise them accordingly. This is why directories tend to be smaller.

Yahoo! is a general directory which covers loads of different topics. There are many directories online that are dedicated to just one subject. This does not necessarily make them more complete but at least you know that all the websites contained within them cover the subject in which you are interested. I will show you where to find some of the larger specialist directories in the next chapter.

Meta directories

A meta directory is not a directory as such in that it does not consist of a database and does not directly index websites. Instead a meta directory allows you to search multiple search engines and directories from one place. Essentially, a meta directory is simply an interface for submitting queries to multiple search engines and returning their results on one page.

A better known example of a meta directory is MetaCrawler which you can find at **http://www.metacrawler.com**.

Meta directories can be great time savers as they avoid you having to visit multiple search engine sites and executing the same query on each. The other advantage is that duplicate results can be eliminated by the meta engine and some allow you to sort the results in different ways.

The one disadvantage of meta directories is that they use the lowest common denominator accepted by all the search engines and directories they use. This means that some of the more complex searches you may want to perform cannot be done with this type of tool. Given that I encourage you to use the advanced search options of the major search engines then a meta directory will not be of help for more detailed searches. If you are just starting to learn about a new subject, or you want to find out the extent to which the subject is covered online, then a meta directory will be ideal for this.

Email

In the early days before the extensive use of HTML and web browsers came along, academic researchers needed a way to locate documents. Several software programs were developed that could do this. These programs could be executed directly by someone with knowledge of what the program did, and how it did it. This required some technical skill.

To make it easier various mechanisms were developed so that these programs could be executed by sending an email message to them. The message contained the commands that the program could understand. Once the commands were executed the program would then send an email back to the originator with the results. After search engines and directories started to proliferate, email was used less and less for searching.

Today there are still many resources useful to the researcher that cannot be located any way other than via these programs. Also there are still many people who only use the internet to send and receive email but may still want to take advantage of the resources available. Email is the ideal mechanism.

Locating resources by email has several advantages. First, you can send an email to a search program and then disconnect your telephone line whilst the program performs a search. The next time you access your email you will have a message waiting for you with your search results. This is a cost- and time efficient way of searching.

Second, there are more and more blind people using the internet. Search engine websites are not friendly to blind people. Very often it is easier for a blind person to use email along with a speech synthesiser so searching this way is a big advantage for them.

The right tools for the job

So out of all of these tools, which ones do I use when?

You should use search engines if you are searching based on a concept or keywords. A concept search is where you find a website that is relevant to your subject and you want to find similar sites to the one you have found. Two search engines that provide this facility are Excite (**http://www.excite.com**) and Google (**http://www.google.com**).

Because of the widely differing results you will achieve from the various search engines it would be wise to use a meta search engine or meta directory to submit your query to multiple search engines at once. This is especially true if your search uses simple keywords or keyword phrases. I would recommend using a meta search engine if you are just starting to learn more about a subject or you want to know what type of resources are available online that cover your specialisation.

Speciality directories are useful when you want to know more about a broad-based subject. For example, if you would like to know more about your family tree it would make sense to use a directory dedicated to this subject.

Directories are particularly helpful for researching current events, finding product information, locating background information for a novel, researching a non-fiction book or learning about a new hobby. A good directory to start with is Looksmart (**http://www.looksmart.com**) which contains over 23,000 subject categories.

If you are performing research in an academic field then again a search engine would be a good choice. I would recommend you start with NorthernLight at **http://www.northernlight.com**.

Recently a number of websites have started to appear that can help you to determine the best search engine or directory for your query. Let's take a look at two such sites; Interactive Web Search Wizard and Smartborg.

If you are looking for the latest information on a particular subject then always use a search engine. Directories are updated by human beings which means they are invariably out of date.

Interactive Web Search Wizard

This tool can be found at **http://websearch.about.com/internet/websearch/ library/searchwiz/bl_searchwiz.htm**. It guides you to an appropriate search engine or directory based on one of several predefined categories (see Figure 3.1).

After you have selected a suitable category you press the Submit button. You will then be taken to a page that lists several sub-categories to refine your requirements a little further. After choosing a sub-category and pressing Submit you are taken to a page containing links to the best search engines and directories based on your category choices.

Let's use an example. I am interested in finding a directory that specialises in genealogy. From the Interactive Web Search Wizard home page (Figure 3.1) I select the 'People' category and press the Submit button. Figure 3.2 shows the page I am taken to.

This page has several sub-categories. The one that catches my eye is 'Genealogy sites that help with family tree research'. I select that sub-category and click Submit again. Figure 3.3 shows the results.

I am presented with several directories and a meta search engine that I can now use to research my family tree. At the bottom of the page there is a link to another page with other genealogy resources.

The Interactive Web Search Wizard has potentially saved me a great deal of time formulating a search phrase to try and find these search tools.

The disadvantage of this tool is that I will only see search engines and directories that the creator of the tool has chosen because they are hard coded links on his website. I will not see new genealogy sites unless the creator of the tool is

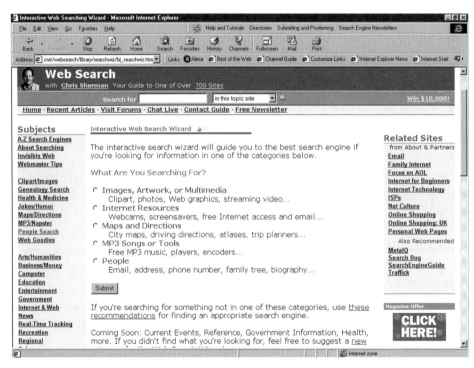

Figure 3.1 Interactive Web Search Wizard home page.

made aware of them and chooses to include them. However, this is still a useful tool given this limitation.

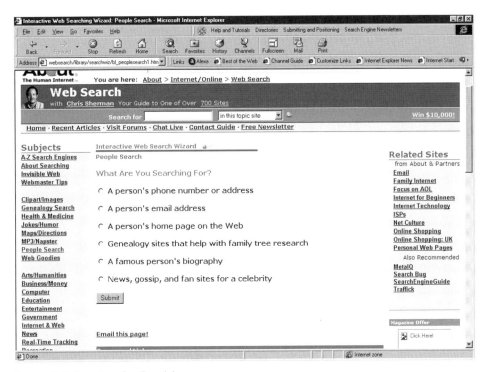

Figure 3.2 Searching for 'People' page.

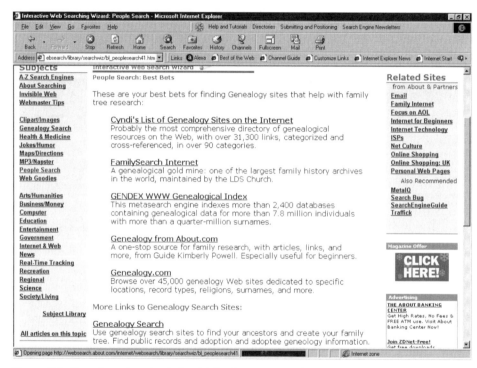

Figure 3.3 Genealogy sites that help with family tree research.

Smartborg

Smartborg can be found at **http://www.teleport.com/~lensman/sb/**. The idea behind this tool is that it analyses your search keyword or phrase and then suggests the search engine that would return you the most relevant results. This saves you having to keep up with the changes made to each search engine which affect how your query is interpreted.

Figure 3.4 Smartborg home page.

Let's work through an example of how to use this tool and then make some observations based on our results.

The opening page of Smartborg can be seen in Figure 3.4.

As you can see, unlike the Interactive Web Search Wizard, there are no categories to choose from. Smartborg will determine the best search engine for your needs by analysing your keyword or search phrase. In the search box I enter 'genealogy' and Figure 3.5 shows the results I get.

Earlier I said not to use a single keyword when using a search engine because you will get thousands of websites that match your query. I thought I would try a single keyword with Smartborg to see what search engine it would recommend and why.

As you can see in Figure 3.5 it has recommended two search engines, Direct Hit and Google (in fact Smartborg always recommends two search engines). Smartborg has chosen these engines because they allow collaborative filtering or quality algorithms.

Collaborative filtering uses preferences to filter out irrelevant results. Quality algorithms select results based on the popularity of each resource. The number of websites that link to it determines the popularity of a resource.

So by recommending search engines that have these features, Smartborg is sending me to a search engine that should produce more relevant results even though I am only using a single keyword search query.

When I click on the Google search button these are the results I get (Figure 3.6).

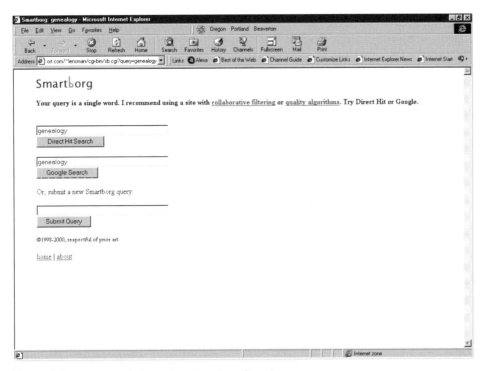

Figure 3.5 Recommended search engines from Smartborg.

As you can see, the sites that are listed are certainly directly relevant but take a look at the top right-hand corner of the screen. Google tells me I am viewing

Figure 3.6 Google genealogy page.

websites 1–10 of over 4 million! So even with a quality algorithm a single keyword query returns an unacceptably high number of results.

Let's refine our query by using a two word search phrase. This time I enter
'family tree' (without the quotes). Figure 3.7 shows the results.

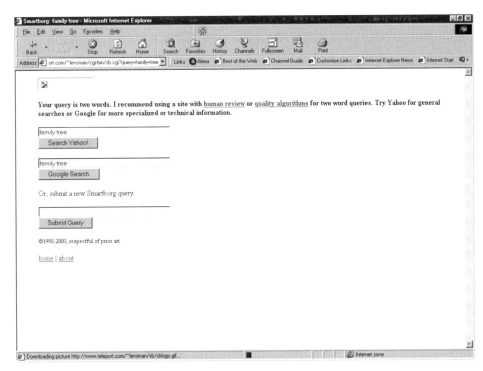

Figure 3.7 Results of search.

This time Smartborg has detected that I am using two separate words and has suggested Google and Yahoo! Google has been selected because again I need the quality algorithm to make the results more relevant. This time, however, Smartborg has suggested I search the Yahoo! Directory because it is compiled by humans and therefore may provide me with higher quality information.

What if I was to enter the same two-word query but this time include the quotes? Figure 3.8 shows what Smartborg returns.

Smartborg has correctly detected that I have entered a phrase and suggests two search engines that support phrase searches, AltaVista and FAST.

This time, instead of entering 'family tree' as a phrase, what if I was to use some boolean logic and use 'family AND tree' as my query?

As you can see from Figure 3.9 both Go and Northern Light have been suggested as two search engines that support boolean search logic.

So Smartborg is a good tool for recommending search engines and directories based on the type of search phrase you enter. I would recommend using this tool if you really have no idea which tool is best for your type of search.

The one disadvantage to Smartborg is that the search engines and directories it considers for recommendation come from a very small list. At the time I tried Smartborg its search tool list consisted of About.com, All the Web, AltaVista, Ask Jeeves, AudioFind, AudioGalaxy, Clickey, Dataware, Direct Hit, Excite, FAST, FTP, GO Network, Google, Hotbot, Husky Search, Infotiger, Ixquick, LEO, Lycos, Mamma, MetaCrawler, MetaGopher, MSN Search, Northern Light, Oingo, Open Directory, RedeSearch, Remarq, Search Broker, Simpli, START, Thunderstone, Yahoo! and ZWorks.

Figure 3.8 Results for the same two-word entry using quotes.

Figure 3.9 Search engines that support boolean search logic.

I am sure this will grow over time but as a searcher you need to be aware that you may not always get the best recommendation.

Search engines and directories

4

How to use the major search engines for research

Search engines and directories can either consume huge amounts of your time online and still not get you any closer to the information you seek, or very quickly they can provide you with targeted sites dedicated to your subject.

The difference between the two is how you use these tools. This chapter discusses the features of the major search engines and directories you are likely to use. We will take a look at hidden resources that the search engines cannot index and how to find them, and will finish the chapter by giving you some advanced search techniques you can use to improve the quality of your search results.

So what are commonly considered the major search engines on the internet? These are the search engines you are likely to use the most:

AltaVista
http://www.altavista.com and **http://www.altavista.co.uk**

Excite
http://www.excite.com and **http://www.excite.co.uk**

Northern Light
http://www.northernlight.com

HotBot
http://www.hotbot.lycos.com

Go
http://www.go.com

Google
http://www.google.com

Each engine will return different results for the same search phrase and each of them indexes the web to a greater or lesser extent. In fact, the percentage of website pages that each engine has indexed at the time of writing (November 2000) is AltaVista 47%; Northern Light 39%; Excite 17%; Go 14%. The other thing you should consider is that some search engines cover particular subjects better than others.

Let's look at what each search engine is good at.

AltaVista

AltaVista indexes around 10 million web pages a day and large parts of the database are refreshed every night. The search engine is very easy to use and many features have been added to make your searching life easier.

Perhaps AltaVista's strongest feature is its ability to retrieve web pages based on specific search phrases. It finds actual words and pages from within the text of each web page, so the chances are the results returned to you will be more targeted. When entering a search phrase you can specify that you want the phrase to be matched exactly by entering the phrase between quote marks. You can use the '+' and '-' marks to include ('+') or exclude ('-') certain words or phrases.

You can search using specific fields such as 'title:' for the title of a web page or 'host:' for a specific type of website address. For example, 'title:familysearch' would return all web pages whose website title contained the string 'family-search'. You can also search with a field called 'link:'. This will allow you to find all websites that are **linked** to a specific website. So I could, for example, find all sites linked to my favourite website. This is particularly useful if you want to find sites that are related to one you have found to be helpful.

With advanced search you use boolean logic. Do not be afraid of this – it really only means that you have to learn how to use connecting words (called operators) such as 'AND, OR, NOT', to make your query more specific.

This would not just return resources that discussed family trees but would also return sites about families and other sites about trees.

There are two other features you will find useful. The first is the ability to enter your search as a natural language question. For example, you could enter 'Where can I find sites about genealogy?' AltaVista would be able to understand this and return sites that are either about genealogy or are directories pointing to sites that cover this subject. The other useful feature is the language translation service. If you find a website written in a foreign language you can click on the Translate link and it will immediately translate it for you. By the way, it is not perfect yet and can sometimes return some very amusing results.

The best way to use AltaVista is to use the advanced search facility. This way you can make your search very specific. In fact, it is always best to use the advanced search on any of the search engines I discuss in this guide.

AltaVista advanced search

The advanced search box is shown in Figure 4.1.

Here's how you use the boolean operators in AltaVista:

- You use 'AND' when you want all keywords in your search phrase to appear in the document, eg 'family AND tree' would return resources that contained both 'family' and 'tree'.

- You use 'OR' when you want documents returned that contain either keyword in your search phrase, eg 'family OR tree OR genealogy' will return resources that contain any of these words.

- You can exclude specific keywords from the search results using the 'AND NOT' operator, eg 'family AND NOT families' would return resources that contained the keyword 'family' but that did not contain the word 'families'.

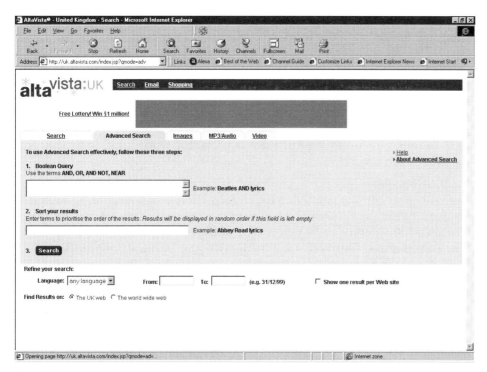

Figure 4.1 AltaVista's advanced search box.

■ AltaVista recognises the 'NEAR' operator. This will return resources that contain all words in your search phrase if each word is within ten words of

When entering boolean operators in the AltaVista search box you do not have to put them in upper-case, but it is good practice so that you can identify your keywords as opposed to instructions for the search engine.

You can use this search technique in both advanced and main search in AltaVista. You can also use several boolean operators in one search phrase, eg 'family AND tree AND NOT families'.

the other, eg 'family NEAR tree'. For a resource to match it would have to contain 'family' with the word 'tree' within ten words of 'family'.

- To get AltaVista to match your search phrase exactly, enclose it in quotes, eg "family tree" would return only those resources containing the exact phrase.

You can also get AltaVista to sort your results according to your search phrase. For example, you can enter '+family tree' in the search box. AltaVista would return all resources containing 'family' with those also containing 'tree' at the top of the search results. So AltaVista is using the word 'tree' to further sort your results for you.

The NEAR boolean operator is very useful. Let's say you were doing some academic research and you wanted to find information about Winston Churchill. If you used 'Winston Churchill' as an exact phrase you would get resources returned that referred to Winston Churchill – a good start. But what about those sites that use Churchill's full name, Winston Leonard Spencer Churchill? These would not be found, so you could be missing some vital resources.

This is where the NEAR operator can help. By using the search phrase 'Winston NEAR Churchill' (without the quotes) you would get those additional resources, as well as the ones returned for your exact match.

When performing your searches, do not assume that your objective is to limit the number of results returned at the expense of missing some vital documents.

Sorting your results
In advanced search you decide the order in which your results are returned. You do this by entering the keyword(s) in the Sort your results box (see Figure 4.2).

Here we are searching for 'british prime ministers' and the sort by box contains 'churchill'. AltaVista will place those sites containing 'churchill' in the results list first.

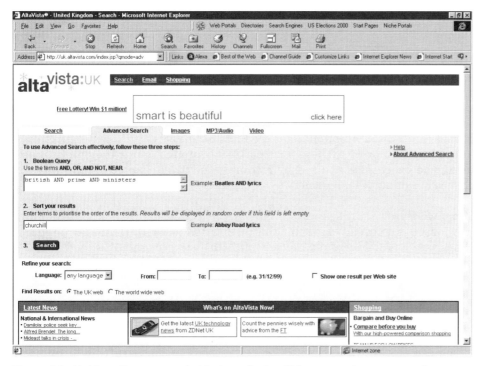

Figure 4.2 AltaVista allows you to decide the order in which your results are returned.

Removing duplicates

If you have done any searching online you will have noticed that very often you will get more than one web page returned from a single site. This can cause you to have to look through more search results than perhaps you would like. To get around this problem in AltaVista you can select the 'Show one result per Web site' box. AltaVista will then display only one page per site.

Using case in your search phrase

You will have noticed that all of my search phrase examples have used only lowercase letters. If you use only lowercase letters in AltaVista, the search engine will match on both lower- and uppercase letters. If you want to force AltaVista to match the case exactly, you should use mixed-case letters in your search phrase. For example, commercial products often use case to distinguish their brand, so if you are searching for a particular product enter the product name using the exact case as used by the manufacturer. You will stand a better chance of finding it faster that way.

Using wildcards

A wildcard is a special character that will match any letter, number or special character. The wildcard character that AltaVista recognises is '*'. Wildcards have to be used carefully as their incorrect use can cause a large number of results to be returned.

AltaVista limits how you can use the wildcard character to avoid you forcing it to search more than 250 million websites! Currently those rules are:

■ You can only use the wildcard after a minimum of three characters. This stops you putting it at the beginning of a word which would cause a search of the entire search engine index.

■ AltaVista will match the wildcard with between zero and five characters only. This rule restricts the total number of matches.

A good use of the wildcard is when you are not sure of the spelling of a word, or you want to pick up both the European and American spellings of a word. For example, 'favo*rite' would match with 'favourite' and 'favorite'. Another use would be to search on both the singular and plural of a word, eg 'dog*' would match both 'dog' and 'dogs'.

Forcing AltaVista to read your search phrase in a particular order
Sometimes your search phrase may be complex and you want to ensure that AltaVista interprets it as you intend. To do this you would use parentheses '()'. Anything inside parentheses will be processed first. As an example, let's say you were looking for someone called 'katherine smith'. The first name can be spelt several different ways and in some documents her nickname may be used. To capture all instances of 'katherine smith' you would need to construct a search phrase that looked something like this:

```
katherine AND katheryn AND kathryn AND catherine AND
  cathryn AND kate AND katie AND cathy NEAR smith
```

This can be simplified and made clearer by using both parentheses and the wildcard as follows:

```
(kat* AND cath*) NEAR smith
```

Another example of how parentheses can help is if you wanted to search for 'road traffic statistics or road traffic accident' you could use parentheses to phrase it like this:

```
(road AND traffic) AND (statistics OR accident)
```

Excite

Excite is best used when searching for information on a specific company and background material about that company. This is because Excite will always return the company website first if you enter a specific company name.

With Excite you can also perform 'concept searches'. These types of searches will return websites specific to your search but also related sites. For example, if you were to search for 'golf', not only would you get sites dedicated to golf but also a results page from current golf tournaments, links to statistics and other key information including news articles and recent photos. The downside to concept searching is you will get a lot of irrelevant sites as well, but among them may be sites that it would not have occurred to you to even consider.

One innovative feature of Excite is its ability to return real-time data. For example, a search for 'London' will bring up the current temperature, a five-day forecast, latest local sports scores, maps and news.

Other features of Excite worth noting are a news section, which provides access to online versions of newspapers and magazines, and a thesaurus to help you refine your search terms.

Excite precision search

Excite precision search, which is available from the Excite home page, can accept advanced search phrases and boolean operators. There is also an advanced search page that provides a fill-in-the-blanks form to make the construction of your search phrase easier, but you cannot use boolean operators. You can get to the advanced search page at **http://www.excite.com /search_forms/advanced/**.

The boolean operators you use with Excite are 'AND, NOT, OR' and these behave the same way as they do for AltaVista. You cannot use the 'NEAR' operator.

You can use parentheses to force Excite to match your search phrase in a particular order. Parentheses work as for AltaVista.

When entering a search phrase you can specify that you want the phrase to be matched exactly by entering the phrase between quote marks. You can also use the '+' and '-' marks to include ('+') or exclude ('-') certain words or phrases.

Figure 4.3 shows the results page using the search phrase 'family tree'. You will notice that Excite pinpoints some useful resources that are listed in the Quick Results box on the left-hand side of the page. If your results page contains multiple pages from a single website, you can click on the 'View by URL' link located just above the search results. This will get Excite to group these pages under one title.

Excite advanced search

Figure 4.4 shows the Excite advanced search page. This allows you to specify multiple keywords and phrases, and whether the resources returned must have, would be good to have or must not have the search phrase you enter. This is just another way of specifying boolean logic without having to know how the boolean operators work.

You can also specify how many results to return and whether Excite should show only the resource titles or a title and summary. You can specify the language you are searching in and can choose specific website domains or countries within which you wish to search.

The boolean operators must appear in uppercase and must be preceded and followed by a space, otherwise they will not work.

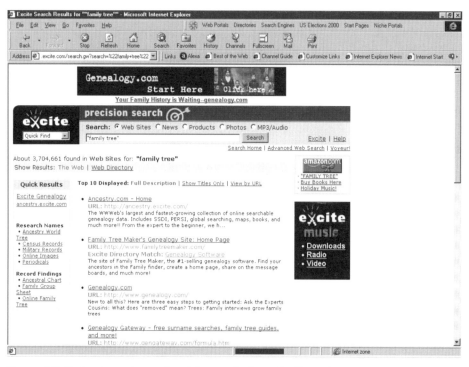

Figure 4.3 Excite shows the results of the search phrase 'family tree'.

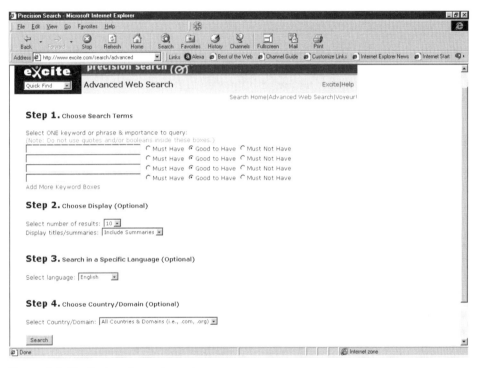

Figure 4.4 The Excite advanced search page.

Northern Light

Northern Light does things slightly differently. Many librarians work for Northern Light and are responsible for organising its site.

It is very strong at supplying newspaper and magazine stories, which are sold from the site. This, combined with its news-filtering technology in its search engine, makes it a useful resource if you are looking for news items. You can perform industry-specific, publication-specific, or news-specific searches.

When Northern Light returns its results it groups them by **category**, not **relevancy** like the other search engines. This enables you to target material much faster and you can view your results by subject, date and/or other combinations of groupings.

With Northern Light you can perform a simple search, a power search or a geosearch. Simple search allows you to perform boolean searches and to include other techniques we have already discussed. The power search is very similar to Excite's advanced search in that it is a form-based search. Geosearch provides the capability to search US and Canadian sites using any part of an address or telephone number.

Northern Light supports the boolean operators 'AND, OR, NOT' as well as quotes if you want an exact match with your search phrase. The '+' and '-' marks to include ('+') or exclude ('-') certain words or phrases are also supported, as are parentheses to force the search engine to match your search phrase in a certain order. See the discussion of AltaVista for examples of how to use these.

You can also enter a question as a search phrase. For example, you can ask 'Where can I find genealogy websites?' and Northern Light will return results relevant to genealogy. Searching by asking questions is very powerful and can save you a lot of time if you make the question very specific.

Using wildcards

Northern Light supports two types of wildcard character. An asterisk ('*') can match one or more characters while a percent sign ('%') only matches a single character. For example, 'kath*' would match with 'katherine, kathy, kathryn' while 'gene%logy' would match both 'genealogy' and 'geneology' (which is a common misspelling of the word).

Field searching

You can limit your searches on Northern Light to specific fields, by entering the field name followed by a colon (':') immediately followed by your search phrase. These fields include the website URL (URL:), website title (TITLE:), the text of a document (TEXT:), the title of a publication (PUB:), a company name (COMPANY:), or even based on the company stock ticker as used by the stock exchange (TICKER:). You can use 'SORT:date' to return resources sorted in date order, newest to oldest.

For example, to search for the publisher of this book I would enter the search phrase

```
COMPANY:"pearson education"
```

To locate a website that has either 'genealogy' or 'geneology' in its title I would enter

```
TITLE:gene%logy
```

You can use boolean operators with field searches so this search

```
URL:gene%logy OR TITLE:gene%logy
```

would find any websites that had 'genealogy' or 'geneology' in either their URL or title.

Power search

As an alternative to the advanced boolean operators and other techniques we have discussed you can use the power search form. This form is reached by clicking on the 'Power Search' link at the top of the Northern Light page (see Figure 4.5).

The top four search boxes work as follows:

- **Search for** will find the search phrase anywhere in a document or on a website.
- **Words in title** will search for words in the website title.
- **Publication name** will find your search phrase in the title of a document (not a website).
- **Words in URL** will search in the website address.

As you may have guessed, the last three searches are equivalent to using the fields TITLE:, PUB: and URL:.

The **Select** field allows you to search in any resources on Northern Light, search only Northern Light's special publication collection or search the whole of the World Wide Web. **Limit Subjects To** and **Limit Documents To** allow you to refine your search query further to specific subjects and/or document types.

Figure 4.5 The power search form at Northern Light is an alternative to using advanced boolean operators.

At the bottom of the form you can refine your search again by specifying a language, country, and a date range. Lastly you can sort your results either by relevance or date and time.

You may find yourself using power search until you become totally familiar with boolean searching; either way these tools will allow you to be specific about what you want to find.

Other useful features of Northern Light

Finally, I would like to point out two other features not found on other search engines that can help speed up your research. Figure 4.6 shows the results of a search I performed using the phrase 'family tree'.

I used quotes to make my search more specific and to force Northern Light to find an exact match; however, it still managed to find more than 430,000 sites. Due to the large number returned, Northern Light has arranged these sites into Custom Folders arranged by topic or type, which you can see down the left-hand side of the page. This means I can now look at the titles of these folders to find those sites that are directly relevant to my search, enabling me to further narrow my results set. You will notice that the second folder has the title 'genealogy' which would be an obvious choice in my example. I find this functionality extremely useful.

The other useful feature is the ability to tell Northern Light to notify me of any changes or additions to resources in my area of interest. If you look at Figure 4.6 just below the search box you will see a link called 'Save this Search as an Alert'. By clicking on this link Northern Light will save my search phrase and send me email alerts when there are new web pages or special collection

Figure 4.6 The results of a search on the phrase 'family tree' using Northern Light.

documents that cover the topic of genealogy. The email will contain a link directly to the results page where these new or updated sites appear.

HotBot

Figure 4.7 The Hotbot home page.

HotBot provides focused search resources that allow you to quickly find resources in a specific subject area. Figure 4.7 shows the Hotbot home page. On the left-hand side of the page underneath the search boxes you will see a list of links to these search resources. So if you are looking specifically for music sites or public records, for example, you can simply click on these links.

Hotbot also allows you to specify how your searches should be interpreted by selecting options from the search boxes. In the 'Look for' box the options are:

- **all the words** – this will return sites that contain all of the words in your search phrase. This is equivalent to using the boolean 'AND' operator.

- **any of the words** – match any words. This option will cause a large number of irrelevant results to be returned, so if you use it make your search phrase very specific. This is equivalent to a boolean 'OR' operator.

- **exact phrase** – only match the exact search phrase. You can use quotes around your search phrase to produce the same result.

- **the page title** – which results in a match only if your search phrase is found in the website page title.

- **the person** – interprets your search phrase as a person's name.

- **links to this URL** – which finds sites that link to the website address you have specified as your search term.

- **boolean phrase** – makes Hotbot interpret your search phrase as a boolean search query. You will need to enter the boolean phrases that Hotbot recognises for this to work. These are 'AND, OR, NOT' and work the same way as discussed for AltaVista.

You can refine your search further by selecting a time period in the 'Date' box; a language; any objects the web pages must include such as images, MP3 music files, video or JavaScript (which is a programming language recognised by web browsers); and how many results to return and how they should be displayed.

You should remember that Hotbot does not index prepositions, conjunctions and common verbs, so do not search on words such as 'and, or, the, is' etc. Hotbot filters out other common words such as 'HTML'.

Hotbot searches are case sensitive and work in the same way as they do for AltaVista. So if you enter your search phrase entirely in lowercase letters, Hotbot will match on both lower- and uppercase characters. If you wish to make your search more specific you should use mixed case, eg 'Coca Cola' will find the product brand faster than using 'coca cola' which will also return sites that talk about the soft drink.

Hotbot also recognises the '+' and '-' marks to include ('+') or exclude ('-') certain words and phrases.

Using wildcards
Hotbot supports two types of wildcard character. An asterisk ('*') can match one or more characters while a question mark ('?') only matches a single character. Wildcards can be used anywhere in a string of characters and can even be used at the beginning of a word, although you are in danger of retrieving a very large number of resources if you do this.

Hotbot will only ever return a maximum of 1000 resources.

Hotbot advanced search

You can select the advanced search form by clicking on the advanced search button on the left-hand side of the Hotbot home page (see Figure 4.8). This form provides you with additional functions to refine your search phrase even further. From this page you can limit your results to within a specific time period, return web pages from specific domains such as educational sites ('.edu') or commercial sites ('.com'), control how many pages to view from one site (by default Hotbot shows only one page per website) and use word stemming to find grammatical variations from your search phrase.

Word stemming tells Hotbot to also search on word variations. For example, if you were to use the word 'thought' in your search phrase with word stemming turned on (by default it is off), Hotbot would also return documents containing the words 'think' and 'thinking'.

Go

Go, which used to be known as InfoSeek, grades the websites and resources available in its directory as follows:

■ **Best sites** – these are the 'best of the best' according to Go. Sites that achieve this ranking must be interesting and relevant, well designed, dense with information or entertainment value, be easy to use, and have intuitive organisation and navigation.

■ **Very good** – these are sites that are rich in content and contain information that is easy to access. Ease of use is also important, as are good design and organisation.

■ **Good** – these sites are functional, informative, and relevant to the topic.

Even though these categories are somewhat subjective, they do indicate that a human editor has taken a look at each site and ranked it according to its

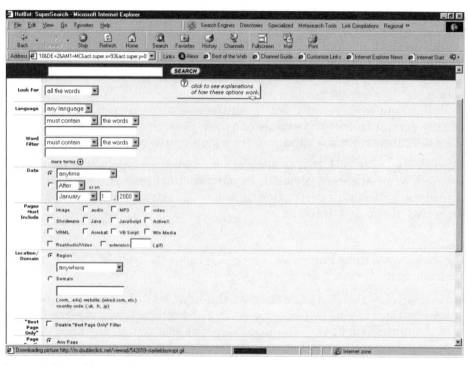

Figure 4.8 The Hotbot advanced search form.

usefulness to a particular subject. Only the Go directory is reviewed in this way; the Go website index is not reviewed. Figure 4.9 shows the Go home page.

All the basic search techniques discussed before apply to Go. That is, you can use the '+' and '-' marks and enclose a search phrase in quotes to get Go to match your phrase exactly. See the discussion of AltaVista for more details.

Go also accepts field searching, so you can search for your phrase in website titles (TITLE:) and the website address (URL:), and can find sites that link to the one you specify, eg 'LINK:familysearch.com' will list websites that link to 'http://www.familysearch.com'.

Search within
Go allows you to return a set of results and then do further searches within that results set. It calls this 'Search Within'. To do this you use the vertical bar '|' in the search box. You get to the vertical bar by pressing the key containing the backslash character '\' whilst holding down the shift key.

Therefore I could enter the following query in the search box:

```
genealogy | "family tree"
```

This would find resources containing the word genealogy and would then search those sites for the exact phrase 'family tree' and return those as a result set.

Boolean searches
To perform boolean searches you do not use operators such as 'AND, OR, NOT' but a combination of the '+' and '-' marks instead. To create the equivalent of a boolean 'AND' you would use the '+' character as follows:

```
+family +tree
```

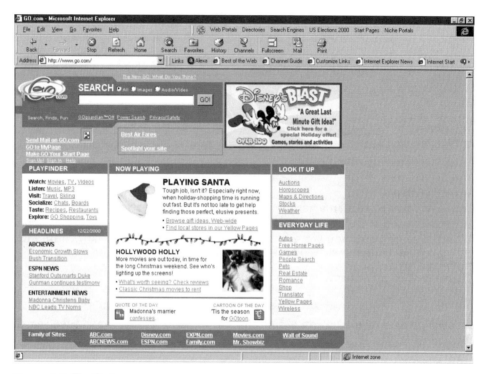

Figure 4.9   The Go home page.

To create the equivalent of a boolean 'OR' you would do this:

```
family tree
```

To create the equivalent of a boolean 'NOT' to specifically exclude a word or phrase:

```
"small dogs" -chihuahua
```

The Go power search

To get to the power search form simply click on the 'Power Search' link from the Go home page (see Figure 4.10). The power search form allows you to specify your search without having to use boolean or field searching syntax. You can select a document, title, URL or hyperlinks to match your search phrase against and can decide whether the phrase must appear, should appear or should not appear. You can also specify that the text you enter in the search box is to be treated as a name or simply as a list of words. You can refine your search to show only results from a specific domain (website address) or you can exclude a specific domain.

Google

Google claims to have features that make the results returned from your searches more relevant. For example, Google only returns results that contain all the words in your search phrase; the proximity of the words determines where they appear in your results: the closer together the words are, the higher the document ranks.

Instead of showing web page summaries, Google displays the area of the page where your search words were found and it highlights them for you. This way

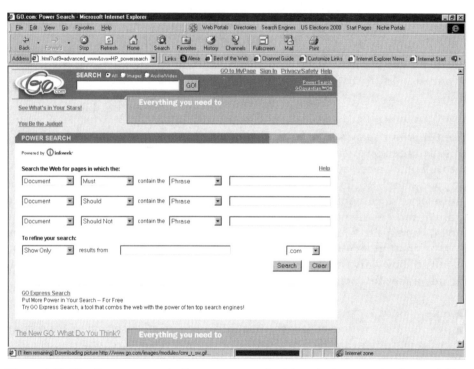

Figure 4.10 The Go power search allows you to search without having to use boolean or field searching syntax.

you can determine how relevant the site is before you visit it. Google takes a copy of each web page so if you click on it and the site is temporarily unavailable due to internet traffic congestion, the saved copy of the page will be displayed instead.

Google also has an 'I'm Feeling Lucky' button (see Figure 4.11). Click on this and it will take you directly to the site that appears first in your search results. Of course, you have to be confident that Google has interpreted your search phrase the way you want it to.

Google uses sophisticated text-matching techniques to analyse a page, and takes into consideration what those pages linking to that page have to say about it – all with the aim of returning higher quality results.

Google ignores index prepositions, conjunctions and common verbs as well as single digits. If you want to force Google to use these 'stop words' you should put a '+' in front of the word. For example, to search for the phrase 'to be or not to be' you would enter it in the Google search box like this:

```
+to +be +or +not +to +be
```

Google does not support word stemming or wildcards. So if you want to search for popular misspellings of words, plural forms or words that are related, you must enter each of them separately. Searches are not case-sensitive so you cannot easily find a well-known product by entering it in mixed case. I find these latter features a disappointment.

However, one feature I do find useful is the 'Similar Pages' function. When a set of results is returned, a link will appear next to those where Google can find similar pages. So, for example, if you find a site that does not quite cover your

You should always put a space before the '+'.

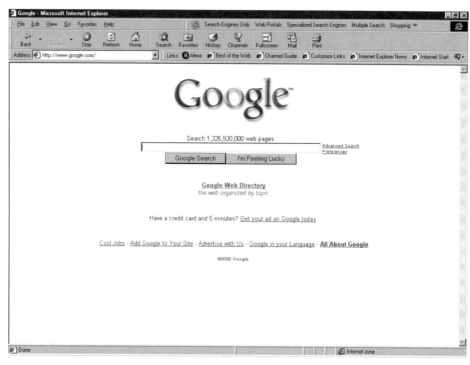

Figure 4.11 Google has an 'I'm Feeling Lucky' button.

subject in detail, you can click on the 'Similar Pages' link and Google will locate other sites that cover the same subject. This saves you having to think up new keywords to try to find those sites for yourself.

Google accepts the '+' and '-' marks to include ('+') and exclude ('-') certain words, accepts quotes around your search phrase which forces it to perform an exact match, and recognises field searches such as 'site:' to search a specific website and 'link:' to find sites that link to the one you specify in your search.

Boolean operators

By default Google uses a boolean 'AND' when interpreting your search phrase. For example, the search phrase 'family tree' will be interpreted as though you had entered 'family AND tree'. If you want to search for either word you must explicitly use the 'OR' operator, 'family OR tree'.

There is no explicit 'NOT' operator, instead you should use the '-'. For example:

```
genealogy -"family tree"
```

is how you would specify 'genealogy NOT family tree' when you want to search for any documents that contain the word 'genealogy' but do not contain the phrase 'family tree'.

Google advanced search

Google provides a form that allows you to specify and refine your search query. You get to the form by clicking the 'Advanced Search' link from the Google main page. Figure 4.12 shows the advanced search page. From this page you can use all the search techniques already described. Google also provides links to some predefined searches at the bottom of the page.

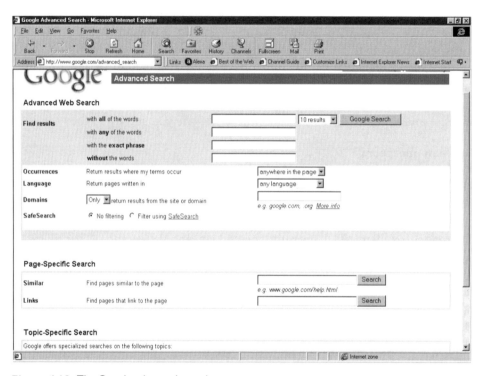

Figure 4.12 The Google advanced search page.

Search engine summary

As you can see from my descriptions of the various search methods and techniques you can use with the major search engines, they all provide very similar facilities to help you refine your search. However, it is important for you to understand the slight differences between these search engines in order for you to be able to use them effectively. Table 4.1 gives you a useful summary of the features discussed above.

Table 4.1 Summary of the various search engines' features.

Search Engine	Understands natural language?	Boolean operators	Special features
AltaVista **http://www.altavista.com** or **http://www.altavista.co.uk**	YES	AND OR NOT NEAR	'+' to include a word '-' to exclude a word 'title:' to search within a website title only 'host:' to specify a website address 'link:' to find who is linking to a specific site '*' acts as a wildcard '()' forces AltaVista to read your search phrase in a particular order

Excite http://www.excite.com or http://www.excite.co.uk	NO	AND NOT OR (must be in uppercase)	'+' to include a word '-' to exclude a word '()' forces Excite to read your search phrase in a particular order
Northern Light http://www.northernlight.com	YES	AND OR NOT	'+' to include a word '-' to exclude a word '()' forces Northern Light to read your search phrase in a particular order '*' acts as a wildcard for one or more characters '%' acts as a wildcard for only one character 'URL:' to search for a specific website 'TITLE:' to search within a website title only 'TEXT:' to search within the text of a website 'PUB:' to find a publication by title 'COMPANY:' to search for a company by name

			'TICKER:' to search for a company by stock ticker 'SORT:date' to sort results in date order
Hotbot http://www.hotbot.com	NO	AND OR NOT	'+' to include a word '-' to exclude a word '*' acts as a wildcard for one or more characters '?' acts as a wildcard for only one character
Go http://www.go.com	NO	AND OR NOT	'+' to include a word '-' to exclude a word 'URL:' to search for a specific website 'TITLE:' to search within a website title only 'LINK:' to find who is linking to a specific site '|' to search within previous search results only
Google http://www.google.com	NO	AND OR	'+' to include a word '-' to exclude a word

NOT	'site:' to search for a specific website
	'link:' to find who is linking to a specific site

Subject-specific search engines and directories

A subject directory is a database of websites, citations and other documents organised by category. The indexing of these resources is performed by human beings instead of software robots, and they evaluate, organise and categorise every resource submitted to the directory.

This process is very labour intensive and as a result makes the directory much smaller than a search engine index. Directories are also updated more slowly when information changes but are useful if you need to find a number of resources dedicated to your chosen subject area without a great deal of searching.

Directories are navigated by clicking on categories until you get to the list of resources for a specific sub-category. For example, if you were searching for information on vacations in Asia you would select Travel followed by Vacations followed by Asia. This sub-category would then be split into many sub-categories, which in our example would probably be countries found in Asia.

To successfully navigate through a directory you need to know how your subject is categorised by that directory, which at first can be rather hit and miss.

One of the best-known directories is Yahoo!, found at **http://www.yahoo.com** and **http://www.yahoo.co.uk**. It serves 50% of all searches performed on the internet and is the most visited site on the World Wide Web. At the highest level Yahoo! uses 14 subject categories which split up into hundreds of sub-categories. It is possible to search the Yahoo! directory, which avoids you having to learn the directory structure to find what you need. This is extremely useful.

Figure 4.13 shows the main page from the Yahoo! directory illustrating the top-level categories where you would begin your search.

Subject directories are useful when you are researching general topics, looking for links to speciality databases, trying to find product information or want to find other subject-based directories and websites. I would recommend using a directory when you wish to find out what type of resources are available online that cover your topic.

How to find them
Here is a list of some of the most useful directories. This should be a good starting point for your search and will help you find other specialist directories and websites too:

- Yahoo! – the most popular directory
  http://www.yahoo.com or **http://www.yahoo.co.uk**
- INFOMINE – a scholarly collection of internet resources
  http://lib-www.ucr.edu/main.html
- eBLAST – Britannica's internet guide
  http://www.eblast.com
- The Internet Sleuth – a good tool to find more subject directories
  http://www.isleuth.com
- Argus Clearinghouse – strong in pop culture, politics, academic resources and other general subjects
  http://www.clearinghouse.com

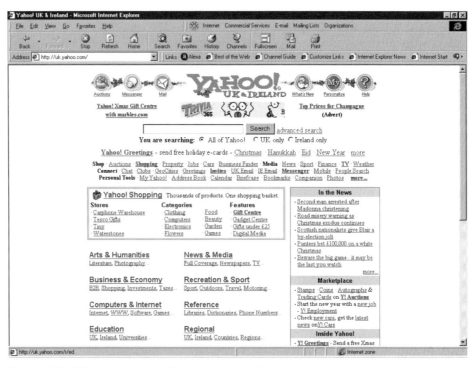

Figure 4.13 Yahoo!'s home page lists the categories for you to begin your search.

- LookSmart
  http://www.looksmart.com
- Magellan Internet Guide
  http://www.mckinley.com
- About.com – covers hundreds of subject areas, very high quality
  http://www.about.com
- Webcrawler
  http://www.webcrawler.com
- AlphaSearch – a gateway to the academic resources on the web
  http://www.calvin.edu/library/as
- Direct Search – a directory of subject directories
  http://gwis2.circ.gwu.edu/~gprice/direct.htm
- Librarian's Index to the Internet – geared towards academic resources and
  maintained by professional librarians
  http://sunsite.berkeley.edu/internetindex
- Open Directory Project
  http://www.dmoz.org

Meta tools

Meta tools access several search engines and subject directories at the same
time and can provide huge productivity gains for anyone wanting to find information. Meta tools do not use their own databases; instead they act as an
interface to several search engines and directories, resulting in more broad-
based searches which can often reveal websites and resources you may not
have come across before.

The biggest advantage to using these tools is the fact that you can search multiple engines and directories from one interface. This is also a disadvantage though in that you may not be able to use the advanced search features found on most search engines. Because of their very nature, meta tools will use only the search mechanisms that are common across all search engines and directories they access.

Bearing this limitation in mind, my advice to you would be to use meta tools to get a general feel for the type of resources available around your subject area and then use these sites to locate more resources.

Where you can find them
Here are some of the more powerful meta tools:

- All-in-One – uses dozens of search tools. A particularly useful feature is the 'Other Interesting Searches' function which provides access to an amazing collection of specialised search engines dedicated to specific topics
http://www.allonesearch.com

- Beaucoup! – access to more than 1200 search engines
http://www.beaucoup.com

- Dogpile – one of the most thorough meta tools
http://www.dogpile.com

- Inference Find – one of the easiest meta tools to use
http://www.infind.com

- The Internet Sleuth
http://www.isleuth.com

- ProFusion – can email you on a regular basis when new sites covering your subject area come online
  http://www.profusion.com
- SavvySearch – good for searching in different languages
  http://www.savvysearch.com/search
- Ixquick
  http://www.ixquick.com

Using natural language

A good way of starting your research is to frame your search query as a question and then use a search tool that recognises questions (or natural language queries as they are known).

During my earlier discussion of the major search engines I mentioned that AltaVista and Northern Light both recognise natural language queries. In fact, you can enter these types of queries into any of the major search engines, but the quality of the results will vary wildly. Out of all of the search engines we have looked at, Northern Light tends to return the most relevant results.

The alternative to using Northern Light is to use a natural language search engine that is programmed especially for interpreting your search query and determining its real meaning. The programming that goes into such a search engine is extremely complex and the technology is still in its infancy. Despite this you can still get some very credible results.

Two of the best natural language search engines I have come across are Ask Jeeves, which can be found at **http://www.ask.com** and **http://www.ask.co.uk**, and Simpli at **http://www.simpli.com**.

Ask Jeeves

Ask Jeeves was probably the first major search engine to interpret natural language queries and to match the meaning of those queries to highly relevant resources. It provides answers from a mixture of human editorial judgement and popularity technology that learns from each question asked. So the more questions Ask Jeeves answers, the more it learns about the popularity of those answers and their relevance to the question originally asked.

The goal of Ask Jeeves' technology is to combine the strengths of natural language parsing software, data mining, a knowledge base and maintenance tools with the cognitive strengths and capabilities of human editors. Additionally, Ask Jeeves deploys patented technology to direct users to sites that have proven the most popular in similar searches. Instead of just counting links to a site, Ask Jeeves' user relevancy ranking algorithms rate websites according to how users interact with their content and services.

Ask Jeeves is simple to use (see Figure 4.14). You enter a query in the search box phrased as a question and then click on the 'Ask' button. The search engine will present you with a page containing other questions which it thinks are more closely related to what you are looking for. You then select the question that is closest to your requirements and click on the 'Ask' button next to that question.

Ask Jeeves will also present you with resources from other search engines that may be able to answer your question.

To get the best use out of the natural language engine you should:

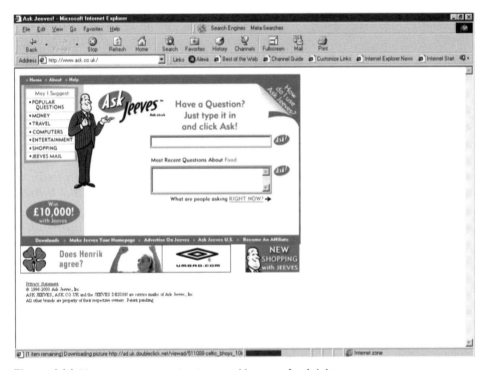

Figure 4.14 You can pose a question in natural language for Ask Jeeves.

- Keep your sentence structure simple and clear.
- Make sure you spell all the words correctly.
- Search for one thing at a time.

SimpliFind™ is the name of the program that performs the searching.

Simpli

Simpli is a natural language search engine that goes one stage further. The search engine utilises principles of linguistics and cognitive science in its interactions with users to place search terms in context. The company claims this provides improved search results for both novice and advanced users.

The search page is very simple (see Figure 4.15), consisting of a search box and a couple of buttons. You enter a keyword or search phrase and click on the 'SimpliFind' button. SimpliFind™ matches the term to a proprietary knowledge-base called SimpliNet™ that automatically generates word concepts and associations. If the term that is entered is recognised, a list of concepts are generated and displayed in a pull-down menu. You are then asked to choose a meaning that will be used to help the search engine understand the original search term.

Let's say I enter the keyword 'genealogy' and press the 'SimpliFind' button. I get a list of concepts returned as shown in Figure 4.16.

As you can see, the search engine has found a number of useful concepts relating to genealogy. If I select 'family tree' and press the 'Search' button I then get a set of results (Figure 4.17).

One thing to notice about the results page is that it contains links to other resources that can help me to further research the subject of genealogy. This is a great tool.

Hidden resources

There are many good resources on the internet that you will never be able to find simply by using a search engine. Seasoned researchers call these hard-to-get resources the 'invisible web'.

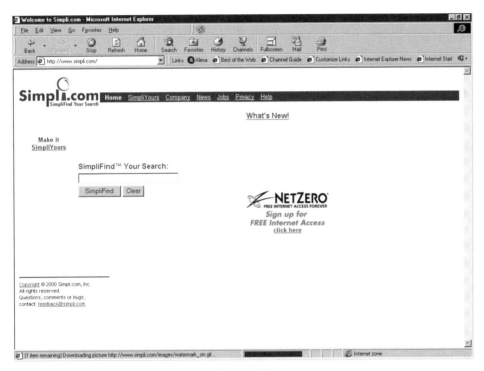

Figure 4.15 The Simpli search page is simplicity itself.

The websites that fall into this category are those that require a username and password to access. The password restriction prevents the software robot, or

Figure 4.16 Simpli returns a list of concepts for the keyword 'genealogy'.

spider, from accessing the pages, so the search engines cannot index these types of sites. It is true that many of the sites provide services for a fee, but there are

Figure 4.17 The results from Simpli for a search on 'family tree'.

some excellent ones that are free yet still require you to register in order to access them.

Other types of sites that are excluded are those that store their data in databases and dynamically build the web page according to criteria you have supplied via an online form. Software robots cannot fill out forms or look inside databases so this data gets missed.

So how do *you* find this information and get access to it? Fortunately for us there are several websites that provide links to these 'missing' databases and provide facilities to allow us to search them. Try these for size:

- The best place to start is Direct Search, which you can find at **http://gwis2.circ.gwu.edu/~gprice/direct.htm**. The site provides links to more than 1000 searchable databases. If you have been unaware of the 'invisible web' until now, then a visit to Direct Search will be a real surprise for you.

- Lycos has been revamped and now provides access to more than 7000 databases, although by the time you read this that may have grown to over 10,000. Start at **http://dir.lycos.com/Reference/Searchable_Databases/**.

- Infomine provides access to around 15,000 resources mainly of a scholarly nature. If academic research is your field, then visit **http://infomine.ucr.edu/search.phtml** – this is a good resource to use.

- IntelliSeek provides a human-edited, indexed collection of highly targeted databases. Visit **http://www.invisibleweb.com**.

I advise you to use these 'invisible web' tools whenever you are researching subjects that are more specialised in nature, such as academic subjects, or you are looking for research papers or you are having trouble finding appropriate resources via the usual search engines.

Using email as a search tool

So you don't have access to the web

What resources can be accessed via email?

How to use email for searching

So you don't have access to the web

There is one tool that almost everyone overlooks when searching the internet and that is email. What, use email as a search tool? Now you have gone crazy!

No, I haven't gone crazy. In fact, there are very few resources you *cannot* search using your email program. Here we discuss how your email program can search online while you are doing something else.

So far everything I have discussed assumes you have access to a web browser and an internet connection. It may come as a surprise to some, but there are still hundreds of thousands of people who use the internet only to send and receive email. Many of these people assume that because they do not have a web browser, or do not know or want to know how to use one, that they cannot access the wealth of information on the internet. How wrong they are.

If you fall into this category, or you would prefer to use your email program as your primary search tool instead of your browser, then what you are about to learn will be most enlightening and will open up a whole new world for you.

What resources can be accessed via email?

You can access almost any internet resource using email. All you do is use simple email commands which you send to a specific email address. Your email contains commands that the email address understands and will execute on your behalf. When the commands have completed, you will receive an email containing the results.

Even if you have full internet access and a web browser, email searching can save you time and money. If you can send an email to an internet address, then you can use your email program for searching.

How to use email for searching

To be able to search the internet you have to send an email containing the search commands to an email address. Which one you use is a matter of personal preference, and which one happens to be working at the time.

Because the machines to which you are sending your email are mostly in educational establishments or companies, occasionally you may not get your search results back. You may also get an email message to say that the computer you emailed does not exist even when it does.

The reason for this is that the machine may be very busy or may not have been available at the time you sent your email to it. If you experience this problem, simply wait a few hours and then send the email again, or alternatively try another email address.

So where do you send your email searches? There are four free software programs that are capable of searching for websites via email – Agora, GetWeb, WebMail and www4mail. There is also a fee-based service called wwwfmail pro. If you want to know more about this fee-based service, send an email to **wwwfmail_pro@wwwfetch.com** and put 'info' in the subject line (without the quotes). In return you will be emailed the help file which explains how to use the wwwfmail pro service and details the costs.

Here we will concentrate on the Agora and GetWeb free services.

A list of the email addresses for each service, together with their location and appropriate comments, can be seen in Table 5.1. These email addresses were current as of the publication date of this book. However, as these servers are provided for free very often they go out of service and new ones appear. To keep up to date with the latest email addresses and how to use them you should visit **http://www.geocities.com/CapitolHill/1236/servers.html**, which is updated regularly.

Table 5.1 Details of the free software programs that can search for websites via email.

Email address	Commands	Location	Comments
agora@dna.affrc.go.jp	send <URL>	Japan	
agora@kamakura.mss.co.jp	send <URL>	Japan	
getweb@emailfetch.com	GET <URL>	USA	Intermittent since March 99
webmail@www.ucc.ie	GO <URL>	Ireland	
www@web2mail.com	URL	USA	Put website address on email subject line. Omit the http://
www4mail@web.bellanet.org	see help message	not known	Send help in body of a message
www4mail@collaborium.org	see help message	not known	Send help in body of a message
www4mail@kabissa.org	see help message	not known	Send help in body of a message

www4mail@ftp.uni-stuttgart.de	see help message	Germany	Send help in body of a message
www4mail@unganisha.idrc.ca	see help message	Canada	Send help in body of a message
www4mail@wm.ictp.trieste.it	see help message	Italy	Send help in body of a message

Now you know which email addresses to use, let's search. In our example we will assume we are searching for sites where we can research our family tree.

Using Agora

To search the web with Agora, you need to submit the URL containing your search phrase. Unfortunately the format is different for each search engine, so you will need to pick the relevant format from the list below. Place each command in the body of an email and send it to one of the Agora email addresses listed in Table 5.1. Make sure you replace my search phrase 'family tree' with your own.

- **To search AltaVista:** send http://www.altavista.com/cgi-bin/query?q=%22 family+tree%22&kl=XX&pg=q&Translate=on& search.x=28&search.y=9

- **To search Excite:** send http://search.excite.com/search.gw?search=%22 family+tree%22

- **To search Northern Light:** send http://www.northernlight.com/nlquery. fcg?cb=0&qr=%22family+tree%22&search.x=19&search.y=17

Enter the entire text in the body of an email on a single line and do not include anything else in the email. If your email program automatically adds a signature to the end of your emails, switch off this function before sending the email. The only change you should make to the URL is to replace my search phrase 'family tree' with your own. Leave everything else the same.

- **To search HotBot:** send http://hotbot.lycos.com/?MT=%22family+tree %22&SM=MC&DV=0&LG=any&DC=10&DE=2&AM1=MC&x=41&y=10
- **To search Go:** send http://www.go.com/Split?pat=go&col=WW&qt=%22 family+tree%22&Go=GO%21
- **To search Google:** send http://www.google.com/search?q=%22family+tree %22&btnG=Google+Search

These URLs were correct at the time of publication but you should be aware that the search engines are constantly improving and adding features. As a result, the format of their URLs may change. One way of finding out the correct format for your email searches is to use a web browser and visit the search engine of your choice, enter the exact search phrase you want to use in the search box and press the Search button.

The search engine will return the results page as usual but if you look in the web browser URL field, where you enter the website address, you will notice that it has changed to include all the parameters required to perform that search again. This is the format you use when searching that particular search engine by email.

Using GetWeb

Searching the web with GetWeb is more intuitive. You simply send an email to the GetWeb server address in Table 5.1 with a single line in the body of an email formatted like this:

```
SEARCH <engine> <search phrase>
```

replacing <engine> with ALTAVISTA or YAHOO and <search phrase> with your chosen search query.

So to continue with our example of searching for sites where we can research our family tree, we could search AltaVista by sending an email to the GetWeb email address containing the following:

```
SEARCH ALTAVISTA family tree
```

This is slightly easier than the Agora server.

The one problem I have had with GetWeb is that I have found only one server accepting this type of query and the service is intermittent – sometimes it works, sometimes it doesn't. The reason is that the server is usually very busy and simply refuses connections from time to time. This is one of the downsides of using machines that are supplying free services. But it is worth persevering.

Getting web pages via email

Not only can you conduct searches on the web, you can also retrieve the text of the web pages you are interested in. You do this by sending an email to the relevant email address including the command shown in Table 5.1 for that email address.

For example, there is a website called Genealogy.com and I happen to know it contains a page that can help me to learn more about genealogy. The address of the page is **http://www.genealogy.com/genehelp.html**. To get this page sent to me I could send an email message to either the Agora, GetWeb or WebMail services containing the relevant command in the **body** of the email as follows:

Don't forget to visit **http://www.geocities. com/CapitolHill/1236/ servers.html** *regularly to find out which email addresses are functioning.*

- **Agora:** send http://www.genealogy.com/genehelp.html
- **GetWeb:** GET http://www.genealogy.com/genehelp.html
- **WebMail:** GO http://www.genealogy.com/genehelp.html

So once you have found sites that cover your subject, you can download the relevant web page this way. All by email, all while you are offline. Very cost effective. Worth remembering when you are performing extensive searches across the internet.

Other internet tools 6

Finding more resources

Besides search engines and directories there are many more tools that can provide access to resources otherwise out of your reach. In this chapter we will consider those tools.

So far I have assumed that you are looking for documents, reports, images, graphics, sounds, etc on the World Wide Web. However, there are other types of resources you may need to access. These can include software programs, historical information not linked via a web page, people, email addresses, reference documents and subject experts.

Very often due to privacy issues, or the fact that the reference material has not yet been linked to a web page, these resources are not available using standard search engines and directories. But there are tools that will allow you to access these additional sources of information.

Some of these tools require more technical knowledge of their user, so you need to decide how useful they are to you in proportion to the potential benefits you can gain from their use.

Using Archie

As I have said many times before, the internet contains millions of documents, many of which can be useful to a researcher. The problem is finding them. Hopefully this guide has shown you where to start looking, and how to look more effectively.

There are hundreds of databases and millions of documents, images, movie clips and sounds, many of which cannot be searched on the web. These documents can be found only by using other tools specifically provided for this purpose.

Many of the tools to find these resources are used less frequently since web-based search engines have come along. Nevertheless this does not reduce their usefulness to us. The tools that fall into this category are Archie and Gopher.

What is Archie?

Archie is a system that will allow you to search for software, data, or text files that are sitting on public FTP servers. FTP stands for File Transfer Protocol and is a way of downloading files of different types from a machine on the internet to your local computer.

Archie covers around 2000 servers and more than 3 million files, many of which cannot be found through a search engine.

You ask Archie to find these files by either giving it the name of the file you want, by using a string of characters you want it to find in a filename, or by suggesting files whose description matches a certain word. Archie will give you the names and locations of the files and you copy them to your computer using FTP. You will need an FTP program installed on your computer to do this.

A program I use is WS_FTP Pro which can be found at **http://www.ipswitch.com**. It has a nice graphical user interface which makes copying files easy. The downside is it costs money! You may be able to find freeware or shareware programs which do the same thing. I suggest you start at **http://www.tucows.com** or search for 'ftp software' using one of the search engines we looked at earlier.

How to use Archie

There are several ways to access Archie. One is to use a command line interface via a program called TELNET, although I don't recommend this because you will need to know all sorts of weird commands and be able to type them in accurately. You will also need to be connected to the internet while you do it.

Another way is to install an Archie client (a piece of software) on your computer and use that. The third way, and the least expensive, is to pass commands to Archie via email. This is a good use of the technology.

By passing commands from your email program you can get Archie to email you back with the files it finds and the names of the servers they are sitting on. You will also have a record of this search in an email which you can save for future reference, avoiding the need to perform the search again.

Before you can use Archie, however, you need to find it. There are several Archie servers around, the most powerful being those shown in Table 6.1. Which one you use is up to you, but it is always a good idea to use the one which is closest to where you are located. Once you have decided, you need to email Archie your request.

Table 6.1 A choice of Archie servers.

Name	Location
archie.rutgers.edu	Northeastern US
archie.sura.net	Southeastern US
archie.unl.edu	Western US
archie.mcgill.ca	Canada
archie.au	Australia and the Pacific Basin
archie.funet.fi	Europe
archie.doc.ic.ac.uk	UK

Bear in mind that Archie is provided as a free service, so its reliability and speed may leave something to be desired. Should you send an email and get an error returned or no email at all, try sending your request to another Archie email address, or wait a few hours and try the same one again.

To perform a search with Archie, send the commands in an email. The email address to use is archie@server, where 'server' is replaced by one of the names given in Table 6.1. For example, if I wanted to use the UK-based server, the email address would be archie@archie.doc.ic.ac.uk.

You can put any number of commands in an email, but each one must be placed on a separate line and there should be no other text in the email.

Here is an example of an email requesting a list of files about 'meteorology':

```
From: gspence@compuserve.com

Subject: (no subject necessary)

To: archie@archie.rutgers.edu

prog meteorology
```

The keyword 'prog' is used to perform a file search. Archie would return an email something like this:

```
From: archie@dorm.rutgers.edu

Subject: archie reply: prog meteorology

To: gspence@compuserve.com

Sorting by hostname
```

Remember, if your email program is configured to automatically add an email signature to the end of your email messages, make sure you switch it off before sending your email to Archie.

```
Search request for 'meteorology'
Host cnam.cnam.fr (192.33.159.6)
Last updated 02:06 8 Apr 1998
Location: /pub/Archives/comp.archives/auto
DIRECTORY rwxr-xr-x 512 Feb 5 21:20 sci.geo.meteorology
```

The details I am interested in come after the line 'Search request for "meteorology"'.

The first line tells me that a computer (host) called 'cnam.cnam.fr' has some files on my subject. The numbers in brackets after the name are the computer's IP (internet protocol) address. The number uniquely identifies this computer out of the many thousands that make up the internet.

After the computer name comes the time and date when the file(s) were last updated, so this gives me an indication of how old the files are and therefore how useful they may be to my research.

The next line begins with the word 'Location:'. This gives me the name of the directory where the files are sitting on the computer. In this example they are in a directory called '/pub/Archives/comp.archives/auto'.

The final line gives me details of the file itself. In my case I have not found a file but instead a directory called 'sci.geo.meterology' which, presumably because of the name, contains several files about my chosen subject. If I wanted to see these files I would have to use another Archie command.

The other command you need to know is 'help'. Simply place this keyword on a line all by itself and Archie will return a list of commands and an explanation of how to use them.

Here is a sample email asking Archie for help:

```
From: gspence@compuserve.com
Subject:
To: archie@archie.rutgers.edu
help
```

Archie can find all sorts of useful information otherwise lost to those who search only with search engines. If you are looking for some facts that have evaded you so far, maybe Archie can help. Give it a go and see what you turn up.

Tunnelling with Gopher

Gopher is a lookup tool that allows you to browse through thousands of documents and other resources using nothing but menus. You do not have to worry about how to get to a piece of information that interests you – you simply select an item from a menu and Gopher will 'go fer' it!

You can equate the functions Gopher provides with those of a library catalogue. You decide beforehand what information you want to find, you locate the relevant category in the library index cards, then browse through those cards until you come across something that might be useful to you. This is the same approach you use when browsing web-based directories such as Yahoo!. In fact, Gopher was an early form of Yahoo!.

With Gopher you perform the search by selecting items from a menu. An item may lead you to another menu, may display a text document for you, or may even download a document to your local machine for browsing offline. Gopher takes care of the mechanism by which each type of resource is located and copied to your machine. All you have to do is find it and select it.

It is true to say that Gopher will not actively search out information for you like Archie does, so to use Gopher effectively you really need to know roughly where the information you require is likely to be found. This is not as onerous a task as you may think. All you have to do is contact a Gopher service and keep selecting menu items until you get to where you want to be.

Where to find Gopher

To use the Gopher tool you can install the Gopher client software on your computer. To find the Gopher software you can go to the site **boombox.micro. umn.edu** and download it from the directory **pub/gopher** using your favourite FTP program. Alternatively you can use Archie to send you the location of the Gopher software by sending an email to your preferred Archie server containing the command 'prog gopher'.

Once you have downloaded the software it is very easy to install – honest! On all machines that contain the Gopher software you will find a text file explaining how to install it. If you are not technically minded, you can access Gopher from your web browser. I will show you how to do this in a minute.

To find a Gopher server to browse, use one of the major search engines – AltaVista is a good one – and search on the keyword 'gopher'.

How to use Gopher

When you start up the Gopher software, assuming you have chosen to install it, you will see the first menu. To navigate your way through the Gopher system you simply select the menu item you want by clicking on it with your mouse. This will either take you to another menu or display a document.

Table 6.2 is an example of a menu displayed by the Gopher server at the University of Illinois. If there are no options on the menu that interest you, your subject matter will be held on another Gopher system. In this case look for the menu item that says 'Other Gopher and Information Servers' or something similar. Eventually you will find something of interest.

To access Gopher from within your web browser you type in a special website address. For example, there is a Gopher server located at Yale University. The machine address is **libgopher.yale.edu** so to access it through your web browser you would enter the website address as **gopher://libgopher.yale.edu.** Notice we use 'gopher://' in place of 'http://' – that's how your browser knows you want to use Gopher and not visit a web page.

The Yale Gopher is a good starting point for your research as it contains links to libraries around the world.

Table 6.2 A menu displayed by the Gopher server at the University of Illinois.

1. Welcome to the U of Illinois Gopher

2. CCSO Documentation

3. Computer Reference Manuals

4. Frequently Asked Questions

5. GUIDE to U of Illinois

6. Libraries

7. National Weather Service

8. Other Gopher and Information Servers

9. Peruse FTP Sites
10. Phone Books

Once you do find a server that contains documents of interest to you, you can bookmark them in your browser or your Gopher client software so that next time you can go straight to your area of interest. When performing your information searches on the internet, Gopher is a good friend to have. It will often find resources not available by any other means.

The one downside to Gopher is that it is not a search engine. Unless you stumble across a Gopher menu item that allows you to search a database of information by keyword, you have to rely on menu items to guide you to the data you need. Also, Gopher servers are gradually dying off as the World Wide Web extends. That does not mean that Gopher has nothing to offer – it does – but expect to be led up a few blind alleys before you find what you want.

To be kept up to date with the latest servers accepting Archie and Gopher requests, go to the Internet Public Library at **http://www.ipl.org/** and select the section 'Internet' which can be found within the category 'Computers & Internet'.

More specialist tools

Now that we have covered the major tools you are likely to use in your day-to-day search activity, it's time to finish this chapter with other tools you may need to use occasionally for very specialist searching.

Finding people

Some of your research may involve tracking down people, subject experts and/or email addresses. There are a large number of directories containing names, telephone numbers and email addresses. Most of the free access directories list reasonably accurate names and telephone numbers, but often the email addresses are out of date, due to the fact that people change their email addresses frequently.

Locating people via the internet can be very hit and miss unless you are adequately prepared before you start. It can be difficult finding a person outside the US as most of the people finders online are concentrated in North America, although over time more non-US sites are appearing.

Before you start your person search you should collect as much information as possible about the person you seek. Here is a good checklist to get you started:

- Write down the name of the person you are looking for, including his/her middle name, their maiden name, parents' names, children's names.

- Write down the last known address, telephone number and job.

- Select the best search tool. Generally, search engines are not a good tool for finding people, unless they provide a specialist people-finder tool. You would be better off with a people-finder tool, email locator or online telephone directory. I have listed the better people-finder tools below.

- When entering the name of the person you are searching for always capitalise each name. For example, if I was searching for 'fred bloggs' I would always enter his name as 'Fred Bloggs'. This should reduce the number of irrelevant results returned.

If you have friends or acquaintances who may know the person you seek, consult them first. It can save many hours of searching.

■ Make sure you use the correct spelling of a surname – this will avoid you travelling along many dark alleys.

If you keep hitting dead ends in your searches, use the information gathered on your checklist to search genealogy sites. You should also consult websites of professional associations as they often provide lists of their members.

To help you get started here are some of the better people-finding tools:

■ **Nedsite**
http://www.nedsite.nl/search/people.htm
This is a great site to start with. It contains links to email address books, phone and fax numbers, names and addresses, missing persons, genealogical records and much more. You can search these lists in multiple countries so you are not limited to the US. There is also a chat room where you can ask questions about the person you are looking for.

■ **International White and Yellow Pages**
http://www.wayp.com
This site provides links to global telephone directories organised by continent.

■ **Meta-Email-Search-Agent**
http://mesa.rrzn.uni-hannover.de
This site allows you to search multiple people finder resources in parallel. The site is based in Germany but provides searches across countries.

■ **World Email Directory**
http://www.worldemail.com
From this site you can search more than 180 million email addresses and 140 million business and telephone directories worldwide.

- **AnyWho**
  http://www.anywho.com
  This comes from AT&T and is one of the best, containing more than 90 million US listings. It also has a reverse lookup where you can locate a person or business from their telephone number.

- **Yahoo! People Search**
  http://people.yahoo.com (US)
  http://ukie.people.yahoo.com/ (UK & Ireland)
  A good people and email address finder. I have listed the US and UK & Ireland sites, but Yahoo! has people finders on all of its international pages.

- **InfoSpace**
  http://www.infospace.com
  Very good resource for locating government numbers. Includes telephone directories for Canada and UK.

- **Switchboard**
  http://www.switchboard.com
  US names, telephone numbers and email addresses.

- **WhoWhere?**
  http://www.whowhere.com
  A good email address locator that works in English, French and Spanish.

- **Ultimate White Pages**
  http://www.theultimates.com/white
  This is a meta directory that uses many of the people finders mentioned above.

- **WorldPages Global Find**
  http://www.worldpages.com/global
  An international directory covering more than 60 countries.

Finding email addresses
Most of the people finders listed above also contain email addresses. Or there is this site that specialises in email addresses:

- **Internet Address Finder**
  http://www.iaf.net

Finding subject experts
One popular movement on the internet is providing subject experts who will accept questions via a website or email and send back a personalised answer. These sites seem to be appearing by the day.

If you require an answer to a very specific question, or need to find someone with a particular knowledge of a specialist subject, then an expert may be what you need. Here are some of the better sites:

- **FACSNET**
  http://facsnet.org/sources_online/main.htm
  This site puts you in touch with think tanks, special interest organisations, government, academic and private sector experts.

- **Sources & Experts**
  http://metalab.unc.edu/slanews/internet/experts.html

- **Ask an Expert**
  http://www.askanexpert.com
  Helps you locate experts in various subject categories.

■ **ProfNet**
http://www.profnet.com

Finding reference documents

These sites are like consulting the ready reference documents at your local library. More and more of them are popping up on the web, maintained by real-life librarians.

■ **Internet Public Library**
http://www.ipl.org
A great place to start looking for reference material on all sorts of subjects.

■ **Digital Librarian**
http://www.digital-librarian.com
A great starting place for all sorts of subjects.

■ **eBlast: Britannica's Internet Guide**
http://www.eblast.com
An online encyclopedia.

■ **Encyclopedia.Com**
http://www.encyclopedia.com
Provides reference material in all major fields of research.

■ **Research-It!**
http://www.itools.com/research-it
Contains dictionaries, thesauruses, biographies, maps and other useful information.

■ **Virtual Reference Desk**
http://thohrplus.lib.purdue.edu/reference/index.html

- **CIA World Factbook**
  http://www.cia.gov/cia/publications/factbook/index.html

Finding quotations

If you are in need of a quotation, or need to find the source of a quotation, try these sites:

- **Bartlett's Quotations**
  http://www.cc.columbia.edu/acis/bartleby/bartlett
  This site is great for finding quotes prior to the 20th century, including the Bible and Shakespeare.
- **The Commonplace Book**
  http://metalab.unc.edu/ibic/Commonplace-Book.html
- **Yahoo! Reference: Quotations**
  http://www.yahoo.com/reference/quotations

Finding FAQs

FAQs (Frequently Asked Questions) are great sources of information if you are trying to get yourself up to speed on a subject, or need broad background material upon which to base a more detailed search.

There are two good sites dedicated to helping you find an FAQ for your subject:

- **Usenet FAQs**
  http://www.faqs.org/usenet
  Usenet newsgroups are the discussion lists that thousands of people get involved in every day to discuss any subject under the sun. A quick way of learning exactly what these groups are discussing and the terms of how you

can participate is to consult the FAQ for the newsgroups you are interested in. For more information see the next section.

- **FAQ Finder**
  http://ps.superb.net/FAQ

Networking in forums, newsgroups and mailing lists

One of the biggest strengths of the internet is its ability to bring groups of like-minded people together. You are probably reading this book because you came across it by networking with other people. This is an excellent example of how networking with others can bring you worthwhile resources (at least I hope you find this book a worthwhile resource!).

When I first came online six years ago I was overwhelmed by the huge number of websites available to me and the bewildering array of search engines that could get me there. In one way I was fortunate in that I was already computer literate before I found my first internet service provider (ISP). For those of you who are fighting with the technology, or who feel uncomfortable with it, the internet can be an intimidating place.

That is why finding like-minded people can bring comfort to you, because you realise you are not the only one who feels lost. And you also realise that you can use peer groups to help you find information you need to complete your latest article, or to answer a question about a topic you are covering at a seminar next week.

So how do you find these helpful online networkers? The first place to look is online newsgroups and forums. You may have heard the term 'usenet newsgroup' used by people on the internet. These are subject-related groups where people meet to discuss a topic of common interest to the group. Newsgroups were the first meeting places set up when the internet became established. You can find thousands of newsgroups online, so you need to be able to home in on the ones that are going to benefit you.

The best place to start is **DejaNews** at **http://www.dejanews.com.** This is a website designed to help you find a newsgroup dedicated to your subject area. It also allows you to browse online the messages posted to the group and to post messages yourself.

Before you post messages, however, it is wise to lurk for a while and see what people are discussing. You can then decide whether you have joined the correct group for your needs.

Once you decide you are in the right place, you should read the group's FAQ, which will be a list of the questions asked by new members about the policy of the group, how to post, what types of messages are and are not acceptable, etc. If you ignore these you may anger other list members with your postings and may start to receive email you would rather not have.

DejaNews makes it easy to find and read these FAQs.

If you do not have a permanent connection to the internet, and therefore it is costing you money to read the postings, you need to get yourself a newsgroup reader. This is a piece of software that will download the messages to your computer so that you can read them offline. This software will also let you join and leave newsgroups as you wish and will upload your postings in a batch.

There are a large number of these readers on the internet, some good, some not so good. I suggest you use a product called **Free Agent**, which as its name suggests is free. You can download it from **http://www.forteinc.com.** I use it myself.

Forums are another place to meet people. They are similar to newsgroups but generally all postings and discussions are conducted on the web. To find an appropriate forum, a good place to start is **http://www.forumone.com,** which has a search engine. You can also find forums by subject.

Another good place to go is **http://www.liszt.com** where you can search newsgroups, forums and other resources all in one go. You will find mailing lists here where postings are sent to your email box every day.

Unfortunately many newsgroups tend to have messages posted to them that are totally irrelevant to the subject being covered. Everything from sex sites, business opportunities and adverts will appear in most newsgroups. However, a lot of the forums and mailing lists are moderated. This means a human being reviews each attempted posting before everyone else sees it and therefore most non-relevant postings are deleted. For this reason I would suggest you participate in forums and mailing lists so you do not have to wade through a sea of rubbish before you get to the good stuff.

These resources will only be as helpful and effective as the members who participate. Those lists that have a moderator who knows his or her stuff are especially useful. But ultimately, the only way you will know what works for you is to try them out. You can always unsubscribe from a list if it does not work for you.

Newsgroups, forums and mailing lists can provide a wealth of expertise and a valuable means to network with like-minded people. By using the resources mentioned in this section, you should be able to find a group that addresses your area of interest and introduces you to people who are only too willing to help.

The biggest challenge for you is to wade through the thousands of groups online. Hopefully I have been able to give you a solid starting point and an approach that will help you to quickly identify your peers online.

Researching current events

A good way of keeping up to date in your specialist subject is to track the latest news. Searching for the most current events is better served by going to a specialist news site. The best sites to begin with are those that collect news items and categorise them.

Start with these:

- **Moreover.com**
  http://www.moreover.com
  The headlines on this site are refreshed up to four times an hour. They are placed into 150 categories, enabling you to view just those headlines pertaining to your interest.

- **NewsHub**
  http://www.newshub.com
  This site is similar to Moreover. The headlines are updated every 15 minutes and you can specify your area of interest to reduce the number of headlines you see.

- **NewsNow**
  http://www.newsnow.co.uk
  If you are interested only in UK news, this site is for you.

- **Excite NewsTracker**
  http://nt.excite.com

- **Northern Light News Page**
  http://www.northernlight.com/news/

- **CNN News**
  http://www.cnn.com
  You can configure the web page to show only news items covering your subject area.

- **Yahoo! News Coverage**
  http://headlines.yahoo.com/Full_Coverage/

Once you have explored these, your next step should be to search the specialist directories as discussed in Chapter 4.

Automating searches

Monitoring the web

Keeping track of the news

7

Monitoring the web

Once you have found the information you need for your research, the next logical step is to monitor your information sources day to day and be notified when any new material becomes available. This way you will always be on top of your subject area.

All online research will involve you finding resources you need and then filing them on your computer so you don't have to search for them again. Inevitably many of your resources will be websites, some of which are dedicated to your chosen field.

Once you have located them, the next step is to monitor them on a regular basis so that you are kept up to date with any changes the site's webmaster may make. These updates could provide you with more valuable information.

You could do it the hard way and visit each site on a daily or weekly basis just in case something has changed, but obviously this method is very time consuming. An easier way would be to receive an email from a site when it has changed. Some webmasters provide a box where you can put your email address so that you will be emailed when a change has been made. However, some webmasters are more reliable than others at informing their visitors of changes, and not all webmasters provide this functionality at their sites.

There is another way: use intelligent software bots. The word 'bot' is short for 'robot', which implies that they are able to do something for you at your command. This really is the essence of what they do.

Bots, or intelligent agents as they are also known, can help you with all sorts of mundane online tasks. There are bots that will scour online news sites looking for news about your specialist topic and when they find some they send it to your email address. Other bots are able to help you surf the internet more intelligently and will even suggest sites that may be of interest to you.

The bots we are interested in are those that can monitor online resources and email us either when a website changes or when a new resource covering our subject area appears online. This can save us an immense amount of time.

First of all you need to find them and learn all about their capabilities so that you can decide which bot to use. To do this you must visit **The BotSpot** at **http://www.botspot.com**, which is the definitive place for locating any type of bot on the internet. The site has a lot of information about bots including what they can do for you and, more importantly, where you can find them.

The best way of utilising a bot

If you are not careful these bots can easily flood your email inbox with hundreds of messages, which negates their usefulness. The point of using an automatic search engine is to get it to return small but highly relevant results.

To achieve this, ensure you do the following:

- Make your search phrase and the scope of your search very specific. It is a good idea to first test your search phrase in a search engine such as AltaVista or Northern Light to see how many and what type of resources get returned. This will give you a good indication of many results you can expect back in your email.

- Do not be tempted to set up lots of automatic searches. Look very carefully at what each bot can do for you and decide whether it is appropriate for your research. It is better to try out each bot one at a time until you find one you are comfortable with. That way you will be more productive when you search through your results.

- When you take a holiday, don't forget to switch off your bot. There is nothing worse than coming back to hundreds of emails.

Here are some of the more useful bots I have used.

The Informant

The Informant is an agent that will use the search engines to find websites that cover your chosen topic. It will then email you with details of the number of new websites it has found together with other websites that have been updated since you last visited them. This information is invaluable because it avoids you having to search the net manually.

To use **The Informant** go to **http://informant.dartmouth.edu** and sign up: it is free. You will be asked to specify the keywords that describe the topic you are interested in. You can also specify particular website addresses that you want monitored.

It is a good idea to get The Informant to monitor some of the 'What's New' websites like the one at **http://www.whatsnu.com**. Be careful though because hundreds of websites are submitted.

How to set up The Informant

To use The Informant you have to sign up for a free account. Your username and password will then get you access to your results. To sign up for an account go to The Informant home page at **http://informant.dartmouth.edu** and click on the 'Click here to sign up!' button. This will take you to the sign up page as seen in Figure 7.1.

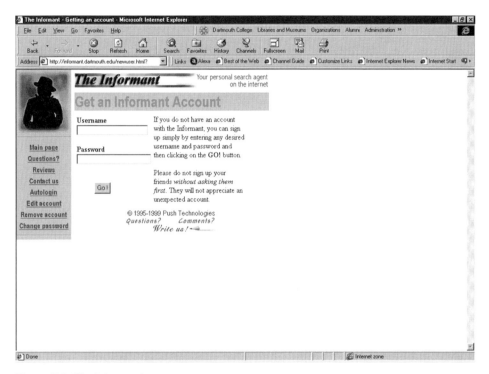

Figure 7.1 The Informant's sign-up page.

Enter the username and password you want to use, then press the 'Go!' button.

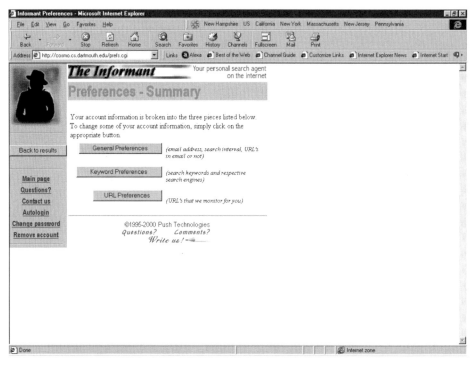

Figure 7.2 The options you have when searching with The Informant.

The next thing is to define the search(es) you want the Informant to perform. You do this by clicking on the Edit Account link. Figure 7.2 shows you the options you have available.

From this page you can select the 'General Preferences' button. This will allow you to specify how frequently The Informant should perform your search, and the email address you want your search results to be sent to, and you can also opt for The Informant to include in the email the URLs of the resources it has found.

The next button, 'Keyword Preferences', takes you to a form where you can enter up to three different search phrases (see Figure 7.3). You should always enter the exact search phrase you want to use and select the 'Match all of the words (AND-query)' option from the drop-down box. This will get The Informant to return a smaller and more relevant list of results. You can also specify which search engine The Informant should use so that you select the most appropriate (see Chapter 4).

The final button is 'URL Preferences'. This option allows you to specify up to five specific website URLs you want monitored. This is very useful if you find an informative website and you want to be notified when any information is added to it.

TracerLock
http://www.peacefire.org/tracerlock/

TracerLock is a free service that allows you to monitor AltaVista for the occurrence of up to five sets of keywords. Every day TracerLock will search AltaVista for pages that match your search term and were indexed three days earlier. The first ten results will then be emailed to you.

How to set up TracerLock

To use TracerLock you need an account, which you can set up for free. From the TracerLock home page click on the 'Sign up for a free account' link on the left-hand side of the page and you will be taken to the New TracerLock Account page (see Figure 7.4)

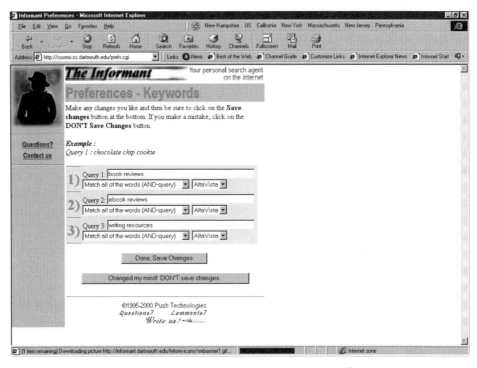

Figure 7.3 The Informant gives you the chance to enter up to three different search phrases.

On this page you enter the username and password you want to use and specify the email address TracerLock should use to forward the search results. Once

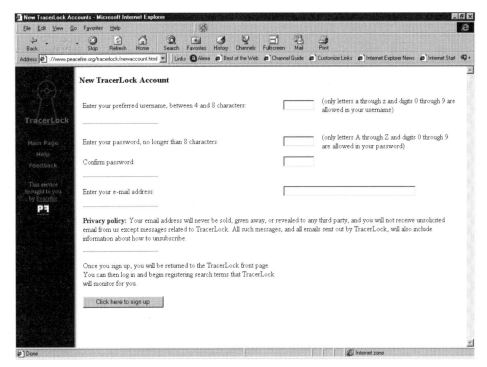

Figure 7.4 On the New TracerLock Account page you can set up an account and it won't cost
you a penny.

you have completed this information press the 'Click here to sign up' button. If all goes well you will be taken back to the TracerLock home page where you can enter your username and password to log in. You will then see the User Profile Page (see Figure 7.5).

On this page you specify up to five AltaVista search phrases and up to five usenet search terms. The usenet searches will get TracerLock to search the online newsgroups for any postings containing your search terms.

When entering your search phrases you use the AltaVista search syntax. In other words you enter your searches in exactly the same way as you would in the AltaVista search box. If you have forgotten how to do this, refer back to the section on AltaVista in Chapter 4. On this same page you can also search the online personal ads and company stock symbols.

When you have finished specifying your search phrases and terms, press the 'Update' button at the bottom of the page and your searches will be saved. You have now successfully set up TracerLock and will start to receive emails within a few hours.

Mind-it
http://www.netmind.com/html/url-minder.html
Mind-it provides a more flexible way of monitoring web pages. You can track almost anything that you can see in your browser, including the entire page, any portion of text on a page, links and keywords. The real power of Mind-it comes from the fact that you can also track password-protected pages and web pages that are built dynamically.

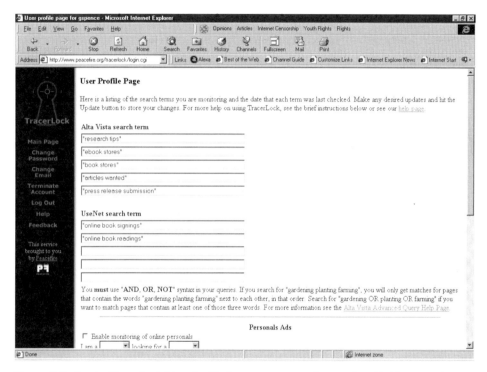

Figure 7.5 On the TracerLock User Profile Page you can specify up to five AltaVista search phrases and up to five usenet search terms.

Mind-it allows you to surf the web as you normally do with your favourite browser. When you arrive at a page that contains something that you want to track you click on the Mind-it button at the top of the page and then choose which tracking method you want to use.

Figure 7.6 The Minder Wizard page.

How to use Mind-it

To use Mind-it you simply choose one of the tracking tools from the menu and configure it according to your needs. When you use Mind-it for the first time it will ask you for your email address, which will become your username, and a password, which can be anything you choose. You will need your username and password whenever you visit the My Mind-it web page or whenever you set up a new tracker. Let's take a look at each of the tools you can use.

Minder Wizard

The Minder Wizard is a tool that lets you visit any website and then determine how you want to monitor that site. The Minder Wizard page is shown in Figure 7.6.

You enter the website URL in the box and press the Mind-it button. You will then be taken to the website you have entered and can freely navigate around the site. When you find a page you want to track you press the Mind-it button in the navigation bar at the top of the page. The Minder Wizard will then guide you through the rest of the steps.

QuickMinds

QuickMinds are predefined searches that are quick and easy to set up – Figure 7.7 shows some of the searches available at the time of writing. You simply enter your email address in the first box on the page and then decide which QuickMinds search you want to use and provide the relevant search word, phrase or product name. The type of search term you provide depends on the function of the search you select. You then press the Mind-it button at the bottom of the page, and that's all there is to it.

Figure 7.7 Some of the options you get using the QuickMinds predefined searches.

Quick Add

Quick Add can be used instead of the Minder Wizard to track changes to a web page. Unlike the Minder Wizard you do not have to visit the actual web page you wish to monitor. Instead you fill in the Quick Add form as seen in Figure 7.8.

The first thing you do is enter the website URL into the 'Enter URL:' box. In the next box you have the option of entering a description to help you remember what the monitor does. For example, if I was tracking changes to the Family Search website I could enter a description such as 'Tracks changes to familysearch.org' (or some other meaningful description). The next box, labelled 'Create Folder:', allows you to specify a name for a folder where the results of any changes will be stored. This is a folder on the Mind-it website, not on your computer. If you are monitoring a number of different sites you may want to organise them in folders to make the results easier to handle. You can see the folders on the My Mind-it web page, which stores all your results.

In the 'Notification Settings' section you specify your email address – this is where Mind-it will notify you of any changes. The 'Notification Methods:' section has two choices: either you have your changes placed on your My Mind-it page, or you get an email notification. Or you can select both options. Next you specify exactly what you want to be informed of: when the web page changes, when the website is moved or when it dies (in other words, when the website is no longer available.)

If you elect to have the changes sent to you in an email you can choose to have the differences highlighted so that you can see exactly what has changed, and/or you can have the actual web page attached to your email so that you can view it offline. To complete setting up your monitor you choose how often you

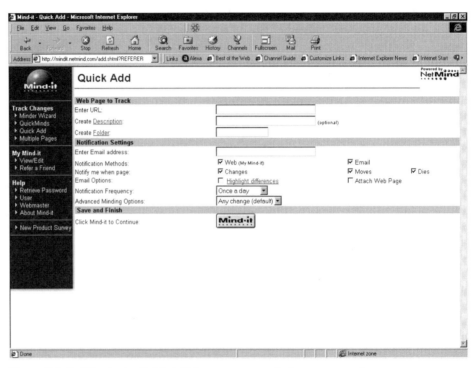

Figure 7.8 By filling in the Quick Add form you can track changes to a web page.

want the website tracked and what type of changes you want tracked. If you choose the 'keywords' option you will be taken to another page (after pressing the Mind-it button) where you can specify either a keyword or a search phrase surrounded by quote marks. Choosing the text option allows you to specify what text to search for. Again you will be taken to another page where you can enter the text you are interested in.

When you have finished you click the Mind-it button and your options will be saved.

Multiple pages

The final option, called Multiple Pages, is basically the same as Quick Add except you are now defining your monitoring requirements either for one or more pages on a single website or for multiple websites. You simply enter each website URL on a separate line in the first box on the page. The other difference is that you enter your keywords or search phrase directly on this page.

Mind-it is a very powerful tool and I have covered only the main features here. I suggest you click on the 'help' link on the left-hand side of the page for a more detailed description of the capabilities Mind-it contains.

Spyonit
http://www.spyonit.com

Spyonit is a very powerful bot. In fact you can think of it as a collection of bots some of which perform predefined searches and others which are more generic. The best feature is that other Spyonit users can share the bots they have defined. So, for example, if you are researching your family tree the chances are someone in the Spyonit community has already set up a bot to perform this type of search.

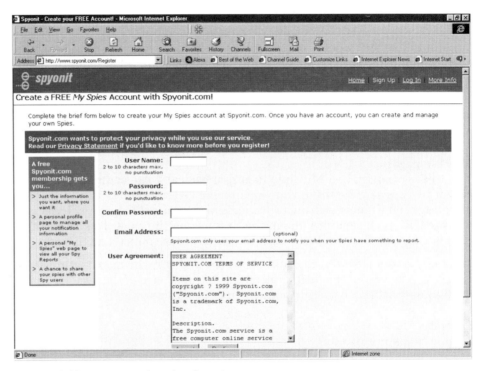

Figure 7.9 You can sign up for a free Spyonit account.

Spyonit bots are extremely flexible in what they can search for and monitor, which makes them very powerful. Once you have set up a bot it will email you with the initial results and will then email you when new resources are found. It also has a vacation button which suspends email to you while you are away.

How to set up Spyonit

To use Spyonit you need to set up an account, which is free. From the Spyonit home page click on the 'Sign up now' link on the right-hand side of the page underneath the username and password boxes. You will then be taken to the sign-up form as seen in Figure 7.9.

Enter a username, password and your email address, then read the terms and conditions and press the 'Accept' button. Your account will be created. Once your account has been set up, you should log in with your chosen username and password. To create your first spy bot you should select from the appropriate category in the Spy Catalog (see Figure 7.10).

The spy bots are categorised by subject and there is also a category called Shared Spies where you can select a bot already set up by another Spyonit user. This is a good place to start. Another useful category is the Swiss Army Spies which have predefined searches for monitoring specific websites, searching newsgroups and other useful search facilities. The 'PermaSearch' bot will allow you to use search phrases and get them executed at Northern Light and AltaVista.

Once you have configured a bot it will be added to your 'My Spies' page. The search results will be collected here as well as being emailed to you if that is what you have requested. If you do not ask Spyonit to email the results you will have to remember to visit the 'My Spies' page.

When you have finished using Spyonit you must log off by clicking on the 'Sign out' link on the top right of the page.

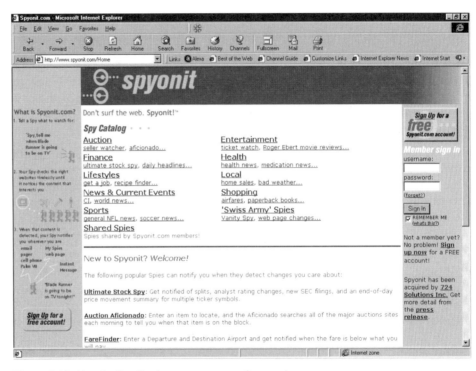

Figure 7.10 Use the Spy Catalog to create your first spy bot.

NET-HAPPENINGS automatic website notification

NET-HAPPENINGS is an email announcement list of new websites. When new sites come online this agent emails you with the details. You cannot target specific topics with this list, which means you may have to filter out a lot of irrelevant sites, so think carefully before using this.

If you wish to sign up, then go to **http://listserv.classroom.com/archives/net-happenings.html** and leave your email address.

Keeping track of the news

Finding sites dedicated to your topic is only half the battle. If you are to do your job properly you will need to keep abreast of the changes in your chosen field. You can do this by perusing newspapers, magazines and trade periodicals, but this can be time consuming. Here again the internet can help.

Most newspapers and magazines can now be read online and even better can alert you to changes and significant events happening in your field. They do this by sending you an email on a regular basis containing news items of relevance to you.

The websites I use are listed below. Some of these will keep you updated for free, others may charge you a fee. Take my word for it, you do not need to pay a fee to get good quality information sent to your email box.

Try these sites for size:

- **PR Newswire**
  http://www.prnewswire.com

- **NewsBytes**
  http://www.newsbytes.com
- **PR Web**
  http://www.prweb.com
- **WebWire**
  http://www.webwire.com
- **Internet News Bureau**
  http://www.newsbureau.com

Each of these sites has a facility to register for news updates on topics of your choice and have them sent to your email box. Once you have registered you will start to receive press releases, company information and news items from the major publications around the world.

Saving your searches

8

The different file types you may encounter

As you carry out your research on the internet you will come across many different file formats. The format of a file determines what type of file it is and therefore what computer program can read it. The format of a file is indicated by what is known as a file extension. On a personal computer (PC) this is always three characters long, (on other types of computers it can be more or less) and always appears after the full stop in the filename.

For example, you may frequently see a file called 'readme.txt' on your PC. A software manufacturer usually supplies this file with their software program and it normally contains instructions on how to install and use the program. The file extension in this case is 'txt' which means the file contains text and therefore can be read by any program that understands a text formatted file (such as a word processor).

There are other files of different types, some of which contain sound, images and movies for example. A complete list is provided in Table 8.1. It is important for you to know the format of a file so that you can determine whether you will be able to read it once you have copied it to your computer.

Table 8.1 A list of the different file types you may come across.

File extension	File contains ...
avi	Video
bmp, pcx, gif, jpg, jpeg, jpe, tif	Graphics
doc	Microsoft word-processor document

exe	A software program
hlp	A Windows help file
html, htm	A web page
mpeg, mpg, mpe	Video
pdf	Adobe Acrobat document
ram, ra	Audio
rtf	Rich text format understandable by several word-processor programs
txt, asc	Text
wav	Audio
wpd	WordPerfect format readable by the WordPerfect word processor and other word-processing prorams
xls	A spreadsheet readable by Microsoft Excel
zip, arc	A compressed file which contains other files. Is read by the Winzip program and others

On a PC running Microsoft Windows you can open any of these file types by double clicking your mouse button while the mouse cursor is pointing to the file name. Windows will recognise the file format and open the file using the correct program for that file type. If one cannot be found on your computer you will get an error message and you will not be able to read the file.

Saving your material

Once you have found a web page, document or other resource you want to use you will want to save it on your computer disk locally so that you do not have to find the resource again or read it online. Unfortunately there are different ways of saving the resources you find depending on the type of file it is.

Saving web pages

The most common file you will want to save is a web page, which has a file extension of 'htm' or 'html'. Web pages are very easy to save. While the web page is displayed in your web browser click on the 'File' option in the menu, then choose 'Save As...'. A box will appear similar to the one in Figure 8.1 that allows you to choose the folder into which you want to save your web page. You can also enter the name you want to give the file (a name will be suggested but you can change it if you wish) and the file type will be 'HTML file', which means the file will be saved as a web page file. You can also save the web page as a text file by clicking on the arrow to the right of the 'Save as type' box and select the 'Plain Text (.txt)' option. Be careful when saving web pages as text files as the format of the page will be changed and may become unreadable.

When saving a web page you should be aware that any pictures, graphics, sound or video files that appear on the page will not be saved. You have to save these separately. The way you do this is to place your mouse cursor over the picture you want to save, click the right mouse button and a menu will appear. From the menu click the 'Save Image As...' or 'Save Picture As...' option. You will be presented with a box similar to that shown in Figure 8.1. You must do this for every non-text object on the web page you want to save.

When saving files **do not** *change the file extension – it may make the file unreadable.*

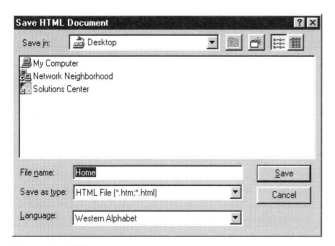

Make sure you save these objects in the same folder as the web page itself. That way, when you open the 'htm' or 'html' file in your browser you will see the non-text objects as well even when you are not connected to the internet.

Figure 8.1 When saving a web page, pictures must be saved separately to the text.

Saving other file types

Many web pages contain links to word-processed documents, 'pdf' files, and software programs. These are all saved in the same way as non-text objects described above. You do not have to click on the link to open the document in order to save it. All you need to do is to place your mouse cursor over the link and click the right mouse button, then select the 'Save Link As...' option.

If you are not sure what file type the link is pointing to just place your mouse cursor over the link, then look in the status bar at the bottom of your web browser. The file extension will appear at the very end.

Compressing and decompressing files

Over time you will collect many hundreds if not thousands of files during your online research activities. These files take up valuable disk space in your computer. Some documents can be very large and it does not take many to fill up your disk. If your disk fills completely you will not be able to use your computer at worst; at best you will start getting error messages and your computer may crash.

To save disk space you should either delete unwanted files periodically or copy them to a floppy disk, or alternatively compress them so they take up less space.

A file is compressed using a software program especially written for the purpose. Once a file has been compressed it cannot be read until it has been decompressed by the same program. So compressing files will allow you to store more of them on your hard disk, but each time you want to read them you must decompress them.

On Microsoft Windows PCs most compressed files have a 'zip' or 'arc' extension. These files are commonly created using a program called WinZip which is a popular compression/decompression tool. You can get a copy by going to **http://www.winzip.com** where you can download a trial copy so that you can see what it is like to use before you buy it.

If you have a Macintosh a common file extension for compressed files is 'sit' which is created by a program called 'StuffIt'. You can get a copy of this program at **http://www.aladdinsys.com/stuffit**/.

These compressed files can contain lots of different files within them so you could use them as a kind of library of related documents. Both WinZip and StuffIt allow you to selectively decompress a single file as and when you need to read it.

Saving your data as spreadsheets and databases

Many academic sites provide large volumes of statistical data that would be unrealistic to display on a web page. Instead they provide a data file that can be read by a spreadsheet program, such as Microsoft Excel, or a database program such as Microsoft Access. This introduces more file formats that you need to be aware of. I have listed these spreadsheet and database formats in Table 8.2.

Table 8.2 Spreadsheet and database formats you should recognise.

File extension	File can be read by...
wk*	Lotus 1-2-3 spreadsheet program
wq*	Quattro Pro spreadsheet program
csv	Any program that can read Comma Separated Values
dbf	FoxPro database program
mdb	Microsoft Access program
db	Paradox Database program

The asterisk (*) after a file extension indicates that other characters may appear in this position.

If you come across links to these types of files you can save them in exactly the same way as any other files by clicking on your right mouse button and choosing the 'Save As...' menu option. To read these files you will either need the program specified in Table 8.2 or another program that can read the same file format.

Most spreadsheet programs and databases can read a 'csv' formatted file. This format is quite common on statistical research sites on the internet.

You may come across websites that display tables of data on their web pages. If you are not sure whether the data you are viewing is defined as a table you can check by looking at the contents of the HTML file that is being used to display the web page. You can look inside this file from within your browser.

The way to do this is to click on the 'View' option, which can be found in the menu at the top of your screen, then click on 'Page Source' (if you are using the Netscape browser) or 'Source' (if you are using Microsoft Internet Explorer as your browser). A separate window will open up containing the contents of the page and the HTML commands it uses. If you see '<TR>' and '<TD>' HTML commands, you are viewing an HTML table. These commands are used in the HTML language to define a table. In Figure 8.2 you can see an example from the US Census website of a web page that contains a table, and in Figure 8.3 the HTML commands where the table is defined.

You can save this table into a file on your computer and then import it into your spreadsheet program. You do this by saving the web page as described earlier and then in your spreadsheet program you use the 'Import' feature and select HTML as the import file format.

Organising your material

Saving files to your computer hard disk is one thing, finding those files again is another! The best trait a professional researcher can have is organisation. Organising your resources can save hours of frustration. After all, you do not want to spend hours online finding all the best sources for your topic and then not know where they are when you need to read or refer to them at a later date.

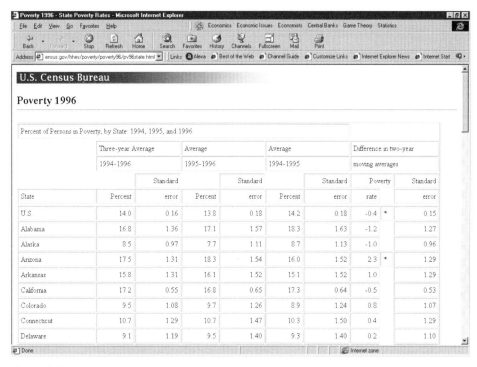

Figure 8.2 An example from the US Census website of a web page that contains a table.

Not only will you need to organise files into some semblance of order, you may need to save links to websites and other online resources too.

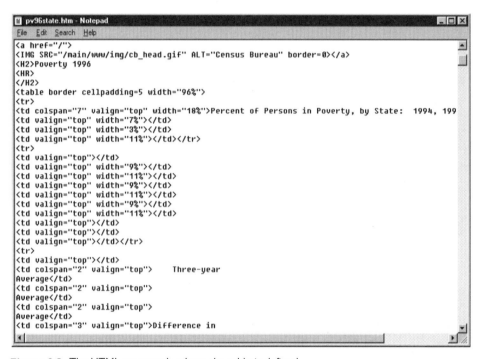

Figure 8.3 The HTML commands where the table is defined.

At a most basic level I advise you to create folders on your computer where you can store all the files you have found for a particular topic. The best way of doing this is to create a main topic folder and then within that create folders for sub-topics. Figure 8.4 shows the structure of the folders I used when organising the material for this book.

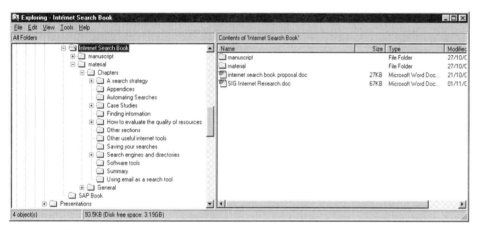

Figure 8.4 The structure of the folders used in the organisation of this Simple Guide.

Organising links can be done in a similar fashion. Your web browser will allow you to save website URLs and present them to you as a list from which you can select when you want to visit the sites again. If you are using the Netscape browser, these links are called bookmarks; in Microsoft Internet Explorer they are called 'Favorites'.

When you visit a website that is useful you can save the URL. In Netscape you do this by clicking on the 'Bookmarks' menu option. This opens up another menu from which you select 'Add Bookmark' and the website URL will be added to your list. In Internet Explorer you select the 'Favorites' menu option, which displays another menu from which you choose the 'Add to Favorites...' option.

Both web browsers provide the facility to place the URLs into folders and I would strongly advise you to do this. You may want to structure the folders the same way as I have suggested for storing your files.

Software tools

9

Software search tools

Any successful researcher will tell you that not only do you need to know how to phrase your search queries so that the results returned to you from search engines and directories are highly relevant, you also need to be able to perform your searches with the minimum of time and effort. One way of achieving this is to use powerful, high-quality search tools.

In this chapter I will draw your attention to several tools – all of which you can use for free – which will provide you with even more powerful search functions to help you get to relevant resources and eliminate unrelated resources quickly.

The biggest problem an online researcher faces is how to find high-quality websites and documents that relate directly to the subject being researched. You can waste many hours filtering out irrelevant and inaccurate resources, which can lead to frustration on your part.

Over the past few years several companies have sprung up to solve the search dilemma by providing software that can search in context, can suggest related subject categories to help you find more relevant resources, and can pinpoint websites that relate directly to your subject. By combining these tools with the search techniques described in this book, you can be sure that you are using your time online wisely and will be able to find what you are looking for with less pain.

Let's take a look at some of the better tools available online.

Copernic

http://www.copernic.com

Copernic is a search tool that will perform searches on multiple search engines simultaneously. It falls into the category of a meta search engine but instead of running from a website you run it from your PC.

Before you can use the product you must install it on your PC. To do this just visit the Copernic website and download it from the download area. There is a free version and a paid-for version of the product. The difference between the two is that the free version has fewer subject categories within which you can search; other than that the product is fully functional.

To perform a search you have to select a subject category. If you are looking for details of a particular company you would select the 'Business & Finance' category, if you are looking for a particular email address you would select the 'E-mail Addresses' category, and so on. To search the web you select 'The Web' category (see Figure 9.1).

Each of these categories contains a list of sites covering the topic that will be searched using the search phrase you enter. This approach saves you having to locate relevant sites in your subject area first, and then visiting each one in turn to find the specific information you are after.

Once you select a category a box appears where you can specify what you want to search for (see Figure 9.2). In the 'Query' box you enter a search keyword, phrase or question, then select how you want Copernic to interpret your search text. The last box allows you to specify what Copernic should do automatically as it finds your results. The options are:

- **None** – Copernic will simply return the search results.
- **Validate documents** – Copernic will check to make sure each website it finds is still available on the web. If it cannot reach a particular website it will exclude it from the results set.

The category list will vary depending on whether you are using the free version or not; you can add more categories to the paid-for version to meet your needs.

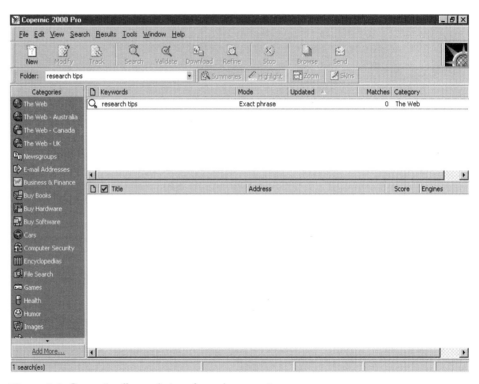

Figure 9.1 Copernic offers a choice of search categories.

- **Download documents** – normally when Copernic returns search results it displays just the links and a description of the resource it has found. This option will cause the web page or document to be downloaded and saved on your computer. Use this option wisely – it can fill up your disk drive rapidly unless your search is very specific.

- **Refine search** – this option will get Copernic to search through the results of a previous search. For example, let's say you searched for the word 'Genealogy', which returned a number of websites. Using the refine search option you could now get Copernic to search for 'family tree' within those results.

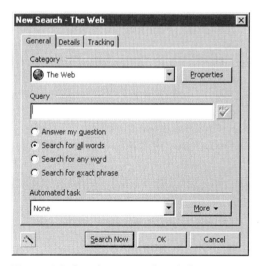

Figure 9.2 Specifying a search with Copernic.

Copernic automatically eliminates web pages that have been found on multiple search engines so you will see only one copy of each page.

Once you have specified your search requirements you can tell Copernic how many results to return by selecting a predefined search profile. When you are ready you press the 'Search Now' button and Copernic will perform your search (see Figure 9.3).

Each of these results has a link to the actual web page. If you ask Copernic to download each page, you can use these links to display each page even when you are not connected to the internet. One other useful feature is that you can save your searches in folders so that you can repeat the same search at a later date if you want to.

Copernic Summarizer

Copernic has produced a useful product for those of us who have to read hundreds of documents, web pages and emails when conducting our research. The product is called Copernic Summarizer. What it does is to pull out the main concepts of the resource you are summarising, which means you get to read a shortened summary of a document that will allow you to check whether it is relevant to your research without having to read the entire document. It also groups the main concepts of the document under keywords so that by clicking on a keyword you can be taken to the relevant part of the document that discusses that concept.

Unlike the Copernic search tool, this product is not free, but you may find it useful if you have to read hundreds of documents each day.

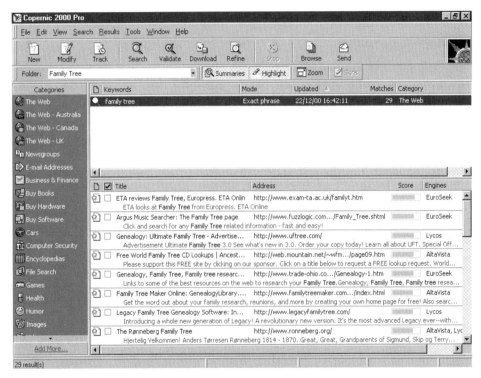

Figure 9.3 Copernic's results of a search for 'family tree'.

Alexa

http://www.alexa.com

Alexa is a product that is integrated with Microsoft Internet Explorer and can be a useful aid to online researchers. In Figure 9.4 you can see Alexa running within Internet Explorer – Alexa is the panel on the left-hand side.

Before you can use Alexa it needs to be installed on your computer, which is easy to do. Just visit the Alexa website, click on the 'Install it' icon, then follow the instructions; the product can be installed for free. The next time you start Internet Explorer you will see the Alexa panel.

To use Alexa you simply visit the websites you have found during your targeted searches as normal. When you come across a website that has some useful information you can turn to Alexa to provide you with more sites that are related in content to the one you are viewing simply by clicking on the menu option called 'Related links'. This can save you a great deal of time.

For example, in Figure 9.5 I am viewing the Family Search website at **http://www.familysearch.org.** On the left-hand side of the screen I have clicked on related links and Alexa has found other sites that I could visit next.

The websites that appear under the related links category are the most popular websites that have been visited by other people on the web. The chances are that these sites will be useful to you too.

Alexa provides other useful information about the website you are viewing, including details of the website owner, statistics about the number of visitors the site has had, how fresh the content on the site is (in other words how often the pages have been updated), any news on the web relating to the site, and other reference information. These types of details would be difficult to find quickly online.

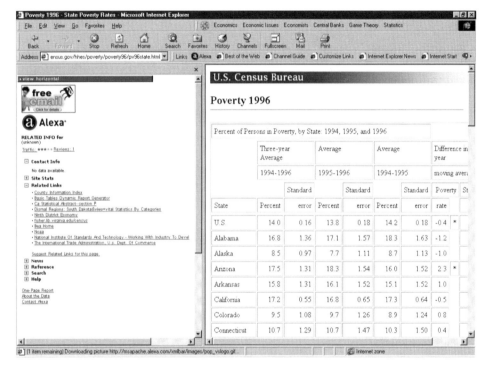

Figure 9.4 Alexa runs within Internet Explorer.

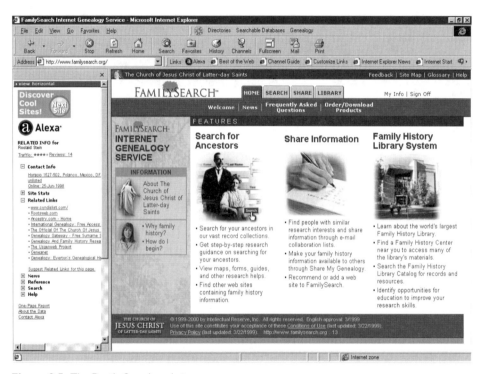

Figure 9.5 The Family Search website.

Alexa can help you to quickly determine the accuracy of the information you are viewing in your web browser and point you to other relevant resources.

UCmore

http://www.ucmore.com

Like Alexa, UCmore integrates with your browser once it has been installed on your computer. UCmore will constantly present related categories of websites for you to consider while you are browsing. As you move from site to site, it will find categories that relate to the content of the website you are viewing and present them to you in a menu bar at the top of your browser. When you click on a category that interests you, a drop-down menu will appear containing links to websites in that category. Clicking on a link will take you directly to that website.

If you click on the UCmore icon to the left of the menu bar you will see a menu that contains various options, including one to visit the UCmore website.

UCmore provides only related search categories based on the content of the website you are browsing and unlike Alexa does not provide any other type of information about the site. However, it is still worth using UCmore and Alexa together as UCmore does provide more categories and links.

Zapper

http://www.zapper.com

Zapper is a computer-based search tool similar to Copernic. First you have to install the product on your computer by visiting the Zapper website and installing from there. Once installed Zapper can be popped up in a separate window and used to perform searches across the World Wide Web.

Zapper is very powerful because it allows you to perform searches in many different ways. For example, you can search by selecting a suitable category and picking a website featured within that category. This is fine for general browsing or if you have a specific problem to resolve. However, the real power of Zapper comes from the fact that it can perform searches of words or phrases copied from any type of document on your computer.

To show you the power of this, let's take the first paragraph from this section again:

```
'Zapper is a computer-based search tool similar to Copernic.
First you have to install the product on your computer by
visiting the Zapper website and installing from there. Once
installed Zapper can be popped up in a separate window and
used to perform searches across the World Wide Web.'
```

What I can do is highlight a section of the paragraph, press and hold down the 'Ctrl' key while clicking the right mouse button, and Zapper will open up with the text I have selected in the search box (see Figure 9.6).

The real power comes from the fact that I can now click either the 'IntelliZap Web Search' feature or the 'Related Sites' feature and Zapper will perform a search *using the context* within which the search words are placed in the paragraph. In other words, Zapper understands the exact meaning of the search phrase based on where the phrase falls in the paragraph. Figure 9.7 shows the results Zapper produces after clicking on the 'Related Sites' feature. As you can see, the sites relate directly to the context of the paragraph. This is a great way to make your search phrases specific without a lot of effort.

Figure 9.6 Conducting a search with Zapper.

I chose to select a phrase from a Microsoft Word document but Zapper can take words and phrases from any program on your computer, including email.

Zapper is very powerful, very easy to use, and free. It can be configured with different search categories and you can even define your own searches to personalise it to your exact needs.

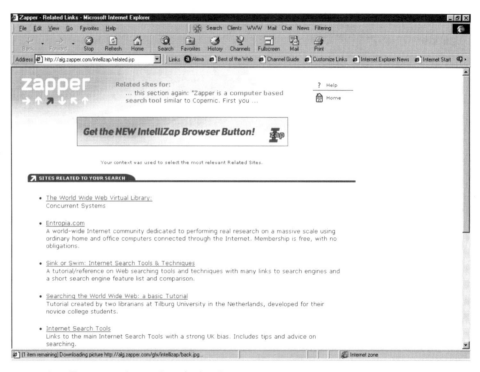

Figure 9.7 Zapper produces a list of related sites.

How to evaluate the quality of the resources you find

10

The problems you may encounter using internet information resources

Practical steps

What a URL means

Establishing the credibility of a resource

Quality criteria to use to evaluate an internet resource

The problems you may encounter using internet information resources

As a researcher, or someone who spends a lot of time online, you will know that the internet offers a great deal of information and resources. Unfortunately you may also know that a lot of it is of very questionable quality.

The ease with which a website can be built and put online for free means that anyone with an opinion, a problem to air, or some in-depth research to share can make it available to anyone in the world. Highly considered academic research sits alongside biased opinion in this thing called cyberspace. The internet has no real concept of quality control. It is left to you to decide what is good, bad, or plain stupid.

This chapter will give you some guidance and practical help on how to determine whether a resource you want to use, such as a website, online article or other publication, is accurate, from a reliable source, and is, above all, trustworthy.

I will help you to:

- Avoid poor-quality resources.
- Assess what is inaccurate or out-of-date information.
- Recognise high-quality resources when you see them.

As a user of the internet it is up to you to determine the quality and credibility of the information you find online. This has become more and more critical as the internet is rapidly becoming the prime source of information for writers, publishers, commercial organisations and thousands of researchers worldwide.

Finding information online is relatively easy as long as you know how to phrase your search query to pinpoint exactly what you are looking for. You also need to know the best search engine to use for your purposes. That is what this guide is all about. The problem comes in determining whether the information you have found is reliable and of a suitable quality to be used.

Let's take an example. Say you executed a query on a search engine using the search phrase 'free reports'. Almost every webmaster will be offering some sort of free report. You will get thousands of website links returned on the search engine results page. Once you start to visit them you may experience the following problems:

1. The first site link you click on takes two minutes to load and then tries to sell you something totally unrelated to the subject of the report.

2. The second site is unavailable because the server is down.

3. The third site looks as though it is relevant and you decide to download the report. When you open it on your computer it contains a virus.

4. The fourth site looks good and the report contains some really helpful information, but it is dated July 1995!

5. The fifth site has just the report you need. You read it and find that it contains some inaccurate quotations. You now need to find another site that contains a more accurate quotation, and so it goes on …

This may seem like an exaggeration, but this was my experience one of the first times I tried to use the internet as a serious research vehicle. Don't be downhearted though – with a little guidance it is possible to find excellent resources online that are accurate, up to date, and more than helpful.

Practical steps

The best way to start is to treat everything you find online with a healthy scepticism and assume that the resource you have found is inaccurate and untrustworthy until you have proven otherwise. You could apply that same scepticism to the advice contained in this guide. Am I writing with authority on this subject? Do the techniques I have shown you really work?

Actually, I have been in the computer industry for 16 years, spent the past six years on the internet, written many technical papers on computing and the internet, and used the techniques you have read about to research the contents of this guide. I may, therefore, be considered a reliable source. I will leave that to you to decide.

This is a perfect example of the types of questions you could have asked yourself about me and this guide before you started to use it as a reference source. This is also the approach you should take to any information you find online *before* you start to use it.

So what practical steps can you take to ensure you use only the highest quality resources around?

The first step is to have a search strategy to determine exactly what it is you are after. In Chapter 2 I described a simple search strategy you can use to get you going. As you become more proficient with your searching you will probably modify this strategy so that it fits the way you like to work.

You should follow up this strategy by using these criteria for determining the quality and usefulness of the information you have found. Moreover, you need to:

- Look for clues as to the original source of the data.
- Ask lots of questions.
- Look at the website address in your browser for clues of origin and authority (you can use Alexa to give you the details of the website owner and contact details. If you do not have Alexa, visit **http://www.register.com** and look up the details there).
- Establish what type of resource you are looking at.
- Ask whether it is a primary or secondary source.
- Decide how relevant it is to your purpose.

An internet resource is useful to you if it meets your needs and is accurate – only you can decide if it meets your needs, assuming you have worked out beforehand what your needs are; accuracy can be determined by some intelligent investigative work.

When 'surfing' the World Wide Web you will be following hyperlinks that will take you from one site to another. Each site you visit could be in a different country and running on a different server. It is easy to keep clicking on links going from page to page, site to site, hoping to find something useful. This is what 'surfing' tends to mean – clicking without a purpose.

If you find yourself doing this it can be difficult at the end of your search to know how you got to where you are and why. When you locate a website through a search engine, for example, you may click on a link that takes you deep into the site and not necessarily its front page (or home page as it is known). So before you spend too much time analysing the resource you have landed on, you should ask yourself these questions:

- Where am I?
- How did I get here?
- Where in the site am I? Am I at the front page, or somewhere in the middle?

To help you answer these questions take a look at the website address, the buttons on the page you are looking at, and look for any clues as to who owns/runs the site.

More specifically, look for:

- A button saying 'home'. This will tell you that you are not necessarily on the front page of the site. Clicking on this button will take you there and possibly to an explanation of what the site is about.
- Navigation buttons – these may say 'back', 'forward', 'next', 'previous', etc. Clicking on these will put the current page in context with other pages.
- A link or button that will give you information about the site.
- A site map. Many webmasters provide these on more complex sites. They give you a good overview of the site at the highest level.
- Whether there is a link to an FAQ – these can quickly orientate you to the site because they typically contain answers to questions asked by previous visitors.
- The URL. It can give you clues about the type of page you are looking at, where it is located, etc.

What a URL means

A URL specifies the name and address of a resource on the internet. It is a user-friendly way of specifying the server, website and web page you want to visit. These addresses are converted to a complex number that computers understand.

A URL contains several parts. Let's take an example. Here is a typical URL:

http://www.info.com/documents/free_reports/report19.htm

By looking at our example URL we can deduce the following:

This URL does not exist, so don't try to visit it!

- It is a World Wide Web site signified by the 'http://' portion of the URL. Other types of sites are file download sites, known as FTP and indicated with 'ftp://', a Telnet site indicated by 'telnet://', a Gopher search site indicated by 'gopher://', or an email address indicated by 'mailto:'.

- The resource is held on a machine known as 'www.info'.

- The '.com' indicates that this is a commercial site (there are many different suffixes – see Appendix A).

- The '/documents' is a directory on the server. By its name we can deduce that it may hold different types of documents.

- The '/free_reports' is another directory, within the documents directory. Again its name would indicate that this directory contains free reports.

- 'report19.htm' is the name of the web page that we may be viewing. Again the name suggests that there may also be a report1.htm, report2.htm and so on, and that these reports may contain additional information of interest to us.

So you can see that it is possible to glean a lot of information from that relatively simple URL, but be careful. The server names are determined by the owner of the website and may not represent the type of information the website holds. For example, 'http://www.lotus.com' may not be a site about Lotus cars but about the Lotus computer software company.

Going one step further, it is useful to shorten the URL to find other resources on the same website. Again taking our example above we may shorten the URL as follows:

Shortened URL	Comments
http://www.info.com/documents/free_reports/	May give you an index of other reports
http://www.info.com/documents/	May give you an index of other documents
http://www.info.com/	Will take you to the website front page (home page)

When shortening the URL notice that we remove the right-hand side of the address up to, **but not including**, the '/'. Shortening URLs in this way can provide you with more information that may be relevant to your search.

You can also use this tactic if you click on a link in a search engine and get a 'page not found' error. Shortening the URL may take you to a website page that does exist and can then help you find the resource you were originally looking for, which may have been moved.

If you want to find the home page of a site, simply remove everything from the right-hand side up to, **but not including**, the first '/'. Other indicators of a home page in a URL will be page names such as 'index.htm (or html)', 'default.htm (or html)' or 'welcome.htm (or html)'.

You may come across a web page address containing the tilde (~). For example:

http://www.info.com/~gspence/

This usually indicates that the name after the tilde, in our example 'gspence', is the name of a **personal** directory on the server. You should then be cautious that any information contained in this directory may contain personal views but may still be useful to you.

This address does not work.

Establishing the credibility of a resource

Before you can determine the quality of a particular resource you need to know whether it is a primary or secondary resource. A primary resource would be one which is produced by the owner of the website and links to and from the resource are internal links on the site. An internal link points to resources **on the same website**.

Secondary resources are those that are external to the website, so a links page on a website which points to third-party websites is a secondary resource. A search engine is a good example of a site consisting of mainly secondary resources.

The importance of a primary resource is that you know the subject being covered is understood by the owner and therefore immediately gains a certain credibility.

Quality criteria to use to evaluate an internet resource

Once you understand whether you are dealing with a primary or secondary resource you can apply several criteria to determine its credibility. The criteria we will look at are:

- Validity.
- Accuracy.
- Reasonableness.
- Authority.
- Uniqueness.
- Completeness.
- Comprehensiveness.
- Information and site integrity.

In Appendix B you will find a worksheet that you can use to help you to evaluate internet resources.

Validity

Validity of a resource depends on how reliable the content is. You need to remember that anyone can publish anything on the internet, so something that appears to be credible may not be and must be scrutinised closely before taking it on trust.

The questions to ask to establish credibility are:

- Has the information been filtered by a third party?
- Is the information well researched?
- Is the resource available in a book format or some other medium?
- Is there any bias?
- Are there any references to documents used when researching the information?
- Is there a bibliography?

Accuracy

Accuracy depends on the correctness of the information contained in the resource. The lack of editorial control on the internet means that resources can range from unintentionally inaccurate to downright deceptive.

The questions to ask to establish accuracy are:

- Has the information been checked by someone else such as an editor?
- Can the content be cross-checked with another resource?
- Is the author motivated to want to provide accurate information?
- Are there spelling mistakes or other typographical errors?
- Are there any references or a bibliography?
- Has the information been cross-checked by the author's peers?
- Is there a date on the document?
- Does the content include sweeping generalisations?
- Does the information change rapidly?
- Is the information one-sided or does it acknowledge opposing views?

Reasonableness

Reasonableness involves looking at the resource and assessing how fair, objective and consistent it is.

The questions to ask to establish reasonableness are:

- Is the content offering a balanced, reasoned argument or is it slanted towards some view or organisation?

- Is the resource objective or are the views presented linked to the sponsorship of some organisation or association?
- Are there conflicts of interest between the views put forward and the author's background (will the author benefit in some way)?
- Are wild claims being made or is emotive language being used?
- Do any arguments discussed within the document contradict themselves?

Authority

The authority of a resource depends on the expertise and reputation of its source. On the internet the source of the information may not be accurately or correctly attributed. In many cases the source is not identified, sometimes deliberately. There are also a lot of sources that are based on personal opinion.

The questions to ask to establish authority are:

- Who is the author?
- Who has published the resource? Is it the author, a well-known publisher, or a knowledgeable webmaster?
- Can a cross-check be made of the author's authority?
- Is the author's email address readily available?
- Why should I believe this author over another?
- What is the author's education, training, and/or experience in a field relevant to the information?
- Can the author be contacted (has he/she provided email or postal address, phone number)?

- What is the author's reputation or standing among peers?
- What is the author's position (job function, title)?

Uniqueness

A resource can be considered unique if it contains a large amount of primary information not obtainable from anywhere else. The majority of information on the internet is simply secondary information such as links to other resources which themselves are secondary.

The questions to ask to establish uniqueness are:

- Does the resource contain anything other than a list of links to third-party sites?
- Does the resource contain any primary information? The 'About Us' link will give you a clue as to the amount of primary information the author has provided.

Completeness

The completeness of a resource means that it is all available online. How often have you visited a website to find that most of its links are inactive and a big sign saying 'under construction' appears on the first page? Would you trust any information on a site in this state?

The questions to ask to establish completeness are:

- Are there any dead links or empty pages?
- Does the information made available have anything missing?
- Is the full text of the information made available, or are you looking at an abstract?

Comprehensiveness

Another important criterion is the comprehensiveness of the information. For example, if you find a resource called 'The Complete Guide to Online Research', does it cover **every** aspect of the subject or is there something missing? Maybe it covers only one aspect of online research such as search engines.

The questions to ask to establish comprehensiveness are:

- Does the resource go into sufficient depth or does it leave many points unexplained?
- Are there any obvious gaps?
- Look at the contents list. Does it cover everything you would expect it to?
- Are sources cited? If so, are they reputable?
- Is there a hyperlinked bibliography of cited sources?
- Are external links for additional information included?
- If there are any quoted statistics, have their sources been cited?

Information and site integrity

Information and site integrity relate to the accuracy of the resource over time and your ability to access it whenever you need to. When viewing a resource that is time-sensitive, it is important to make sure that the information is updated when needed. There is no point using a resource that is five years old if it covers a topic such as computers, for example. Technology is changing almost monthly, therefore any sources covering this topic must be no more than a few months old.

Similarly, you do not want websites to suddenly disappear, or for reports to be deleted from a site, so site integrity is also important.

The questions to ask to establish information and site integrity are:

- Is the resource being updated regularly? Look for the date it was last updated.
- Are there any statements on the site about how frequently the information is supposed to be updated?
- Is there any archive information on the site?
- How frequently are documents moved to the archive area of the site?
- Is there a website version number or last updated date?
- Are all the links on the site still active?

When using the internet for your research it is important to remember that the quality of the information you find and use is as important as finding it in the first place. Your research online can be a productive and rewarding experience as long as you remember to apply the criteria described in this chapter to evaluate the value and accuracy of every resource you find. Don't forget to use the checklist in Appendix B to help you with this process and remember, never depend on any one source of information.

Case study 11

Researching a family tree

Researching a family tree

Now that you have a better understanding of the search tools available to you and how to use them, I will take you through a case study to show you how to use the search strategy, combined with these tools, to find relevant resources quickly and easily. In this case study I will research part of a fictitious family tree.

To keep things simple I am assuming that I have just started to research this fictitious family tree. I have decided that I will follow the family line on the male side. The information I am starting with is as follows:

- I am searching for the family name of 'Waters'.
- I am looking for any people with that surname who live, or have lived, in Yorkshire.

Before I go online I need to plan how I am going to perform my search, so I use the Search Strategy worksheet, which can be found in Appendix B. To show you how I would fill out the worksheet, I have included below each question from the worksheet, my answer to each question, and an explanation of the answer I have given. Once I start my search I may change or add information to the worksheet as I learn more from my initial search results. This is perfectly normal as the worksheet is designed to be a working document that provides me with initial guidance to get started.

Filling in the worksheet

Here are the answers to the worksheet questions:

Who or what are you searching for?

1. What type of information do you need (eg statistics, background information, sources, information about a particular person)?

   Information about the family name Waters, especially any people who live, or have lived, in Yorkshire. I would like to limit my search to UK only

This first answer helps me to clarify exactly what I am looking for before I start to search. Defining my goal will help me avoid meandering from website to website with no real purpose and therefore potentially wasting a lot of time. My answer assumes that I already have an idea where my family was based in the UK, which is why I am limiting my search to people associated with Yorkshire.

2. What type of resources would be helpful to you (eg reports, articles, government records)?

   Census records, any research of the surname by the Church of Latter Day Saints, birth, marriage and death certificates

This question helps me to determine what type of resources I want to find so that I can quickly eliminate any resources which do not meet these requirements.

> 3. Are there any recognised experts in your subject area you could consult directly online? Do they have a website?

I do not know of any experts in my field at this stage.

> 4. What are you trying to do (eg confirm a fact, find new information for the first time, add to your knowledge of a subject, etc)?
>
> **Find any relatives with a surname Waters in order to complete my family tree**

The purpose of this question is to help me clarify where I am in the research process. For example, have I just started to research my subject, or am I doing some follow-up research based on previous results? This answer will help me to limit the breadth of my search.

> 5. Is the information you are seeking likely to be available online? If it is confidential, you may not be able to find it.
>
> **Yes, it is online**

This question gets me to think about whether the information I am searching for is likely to be available online. While the answer to this question will be yes in a lot of cases, you should think carefully about whether your subject matter lends itself to be disseminated online. If you are not sure, assume that it does until you have exhausted all possible avenues.

> 6. Which search tool is most appropriate for your needs (tick the one you will use)? Refer to Chapters 3 and 4 to help you decide.
>
> _ ✓ _ Interactive Web Search Wizard
>
> http://websearch.about.com/internet/websearch/library/searchwiz/bl_searchwiz.htm

Question 6 encourages me to think about which search tool is most appropriate for my needs. You should refer to Chapters 3 and 4 before deciding. Of course, I may use some of the other search engines listed on the worksheet if I find the one I have chosen does not produce any satisfactory results.

The first six questions help me to define the purpose of my online search. The next section of the worksheet helps me define the sources where I can find what I am looking for.

What source will help you?

1. Could any particular company, association, or specialist organisation hold the information you are looking for? Very often you may need to visit only one site to find what you need, especially if that site is dedicated to your search topic.

   List the names of possible organisations here.

   Church of Latter Day Saints, Genealogical Society, Family Record Centre, Public Record Office

Here I have listed some of the organisations I know of that may be able to help. I know of these because I have friends who have researched their family tree and found these sources to be helpful. When you research your subject for the first time you may not know of such organisations so you may leave this question blank. You will come across these resources when you perform other searches.

---

2. Before trying the larger directories and search engines, try to guess the website address of the company, association or organisation. Start with **www.nameofcompany.com.** If it is a government site, **www.nameofagency.gov** may get you there. If it is a defence establishment, '.mil' will be useful. In other countries you will need to also use '.co.uk' for the UK, '.de' for Germany, etc. See Appendix A for a full list of URL extensions by country and type of domain.

Name of organisation, association, etc	Possible name of website
Church of Latter Day Saints	http://www.familysearch.org
Genealogical Society	http://www.genealogicalsociety.org
Family Record Centre	http://www.frc.org.uk
Public Record Office	http://www.pro.gov.uk

I have taken a guess at the website address of the Genealogical Society and the Family Record Centre. These addresses may be wrong but I will not know until I perform my search. If any of these addresses are wrong I will need to use a search engine to find them.

3. If you have found a site that sort of covers what you want but does not satisfy you totally, check to see who is linking to the site. Go to **http://www.altavista.com** and enter in the search box 'link:nameofsite.com' (or .gov, or .mil, etc). This will give you a list of similar sites you can now visit. Of course, you can use this method to also find out who is linking to them and so on. Another site that is useful for this is LinkPopularity which can be found at **http://www.linkpopularity.com.** This will search multiple search engines for links to the website you have entered.

This is an optional question that I can fill in during my searching if I need to. It helps me to find similar websites to those that have helped me so far.

4. If you were not able to guess the name of a suitable site, go to a directory such as Yahoo! **(http://www.yahoo.com)** and browse by your subject category. Visit the sites listed but also make a note of the sub-categories you selected in the space below to get to them. They can be used as keywords in the search engines to find even more sites.

If I could not guess the name of a website for any of the organisations I am looking for, or if the name I guessed was wrong, I can use this question to help me find those sites. I will not use this question unless I have guessed some sites incorrectly.

> 5. If you are looking for product information, use a specialised subject directory instead of a general directory.

I am not looking for information about products at the moment so I can ignore this question. I may revisit this question if I decide I need some software to help me organise all the information I gather about my family tree.

> 6. If you are looking for background information in your subject, use one or more of these meta tools.

I am not looking to understand what 'genealogy' is all about, so I can ignore this question.

> 7. Go to Ask Jeeves (http://www.ask.com or http://www.ask.co.uk), Simpli (http://www.simpli.com) or Northern Light (http://www.northernlight.com) and enter your search as a question such as 'Where can I find information about genealogy?'. This will return a mixture of websites, subject directories and other resources you can explore.
>
> List the questions you will enter into Ask Jeeves, Simpli or Northern Light here.
>
> **Where can I find information about the waters family tree?** _____
>
> **Where can I find information about researching a family tree?** _____

Question 7 helps me to phrase suitable questions that I can enter into the natural language search engines Ask Jeeves, Simpli and Northern Light. Using these questions I should be able to find more genealogical resources if I need them. I can list these resources on the worksheet so I can refer to them later on.

8. If you still have not found what you are looking for, enter your search keywords listed above (written down from your directory browsing) in the major search engines. **Do not enter single words** in the search box. You will get too many websites and become overwhelmed. Instead **enter a search phrase**. Try to make your search phrase as narrow as possible. If you do not get any sites returned, broaden your search slightly until you do.

If I am stuck, this question will help me to find sites I may have missed so far. Hopefully I won't need to answer this question.

9. If you are looking for academic resources such as research papers, or all other avenues have failed, try one or more of these 'invisible web' search tools.

This question does not apply to my current search although I may use some of the tools listed on the worksheet if I get really stuck.

Additional notes

_____

_____

_____

_____

The additional notes section of the worksheet can be used to make any notes or comments as I progress my search.

Now that I have completed the worksheet as far as I can at this time I can go online and perform my search according to the information I have entered. When I have completed my searches the worksheet will be a good source of further resources I can use and will also act as a history of what I have done in case I need to revisit some of these sites.

How to perform the search
The first thing to do is to go to the organisations I have listed by visiting the website addresses I guessed.

First let's visit the Church of Latter Day Saints. The website I get to when I enter the address is shown in Figure 11.1.

Bearing in mind I am looking for ancestors with the surname Waters, I look under the section entitled 'Search for Ancestors' and click on the first link, 'Search for your ancestors in our vast record collections'. I am taken to the page containing a search form.

Figure 11.1 Paying a visit to the Church of the Latter Day Saints.

In Figure 11.2 I have entered a last name of 'waters' and have selected 'England' as the country. When I click on the search button the results shown in Figure 11.3 are returned.

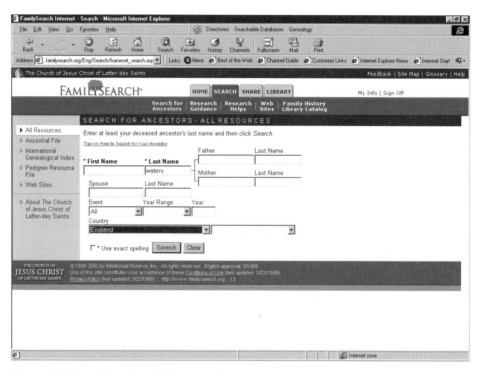

Figure 11.2 Family Search will help you find your ancestors – or anybody else's for that matter.

I have scrolled the screen down to the name of one person who was born in Yorkshire – this looks promising! Clicking on that person's name gives me

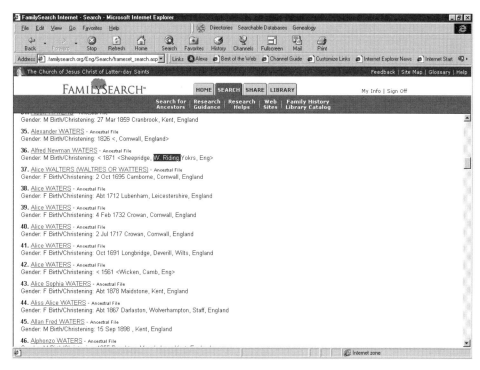

Figure 11.3 Tracking down the Waters family in Yorkshire.

more details about him (shown in Figure 11.4) and if I click on the family button to the right of the page I get some more information about him and his

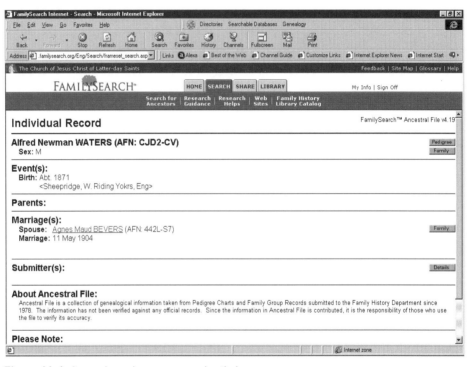

Figure 11.4 A search can become more detailed as you go on.

wife (see Figure 11.5). Now I could do some more research on these names to see if they are the people I am looking for.

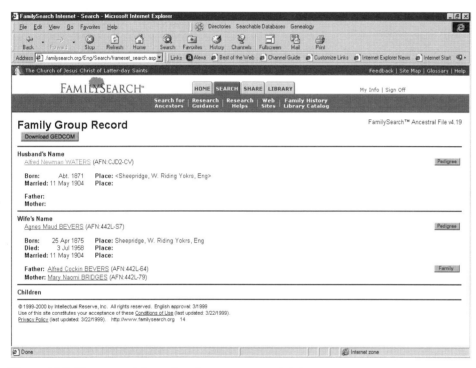

Figure 11.5 You can get information about a person and their spouse.

So as you can see, by planning my search I have already found what appear to be some relevant facts about the Waters family in Yorkshire. This has been achieved by focusing on a site provided by an organisation that specialises in family tree research.

The next step is to check out the websites of the other organisations on my worksheet. Let's start with the Genealogical Society. If you remember, I guessed its website address, but when I entered it into my browser I got a message telling me that the website I entered does not exist (see Figure 11.6). I know there is a Genealogical Society, so the options I have to find it are either to look in a directory and search for it by category or to go to an appropriate search engine and look for it that way.

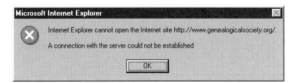

Figure 11.6 If a website does not exist, your browser will tell you that it could not open the site.

The worksheet's question 4 under 'What sources will help you?' is useful here. If I use a directory I should enter the subject categories I used on the worksheet so I can use them again as search keywords if I need to. I decide to visit the Yahoo! UK site because I can view the directory either by category or by using a search phrase. I decide to use the search phrase 'Genealogical Society' and I select to search UK sites only. Notice I am using an exact phrase, as indicated by the quotes, and I am capitalising each word because I am searching for a name. The results Yahoo! returns are shown in Figure 11.7.

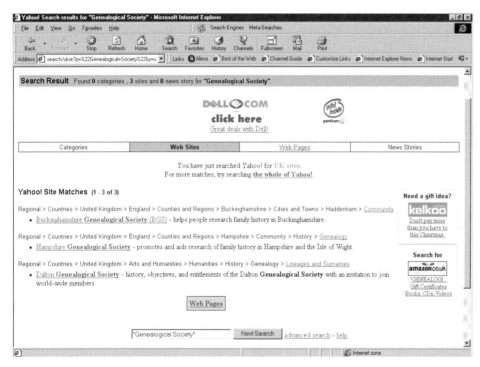

Figure 11.7 Yahoo!'s results for a search on 'Genealogical Society'.

You will notice that I have found three regional genealogical societies, none of which appears to be relevant to my search as they may not cover Yorkshire. I would have to select each link in turn to check their relevance before finally dismissing them. Yahoo! also shows me the categories under which they are listed, so I can put these on my worksheet in case I need to use them again.

However, I have still not found the Genealogical Society. I decide to re-phrase the search query so instead of searching for 'Genealogical Society' I use the search phrase 'The Society of Genealogists'. This time I find what I am looking for (see Figure 11.8).

I click on the 'Society of Genealogists' link and reach the site I have been searching for. I happen to notice it is closing for refurbishment (see Figure 11.9) so I need to get there fast. Don't worry – by the time this guide reaches the bookshelves the building will be open again.

I will now look for the Family Record Centre. Again I guessed the website name but when I entered the site in my browser I got the site shown in Figure 11.10. It looks as though my guess was wrong. However, I have better luck with the Public Record Office (Figure 11.11).

I click on the Family History graphic on the left-hand side of the page and I am taken to a page where I can continue my search (see Figure 11.12). You will notice on this page that the Public Record Office has thoughtfully included a link to the Family Records Centre (Figure 11.13) so I do not have to search for this site separately. Often you will find other sites this way especially if you have planned your search before going online.

Unfortunately I do not have the space to continue my family tree research in detail in this book. However, this short example has shown you that with a little planning it is possible to get relevant results very early on in your searching without having to plough your way through thousands of irrelevant website listings first.

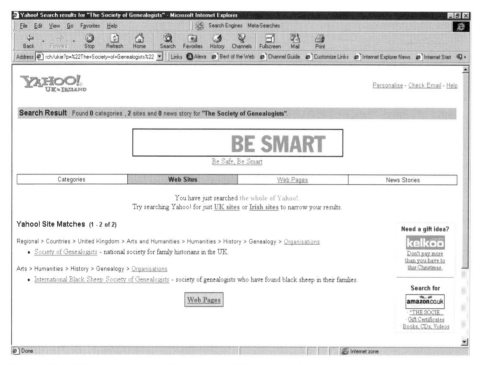

Figure 11.8 The search phrase 'The Society of Genealogists' is spot on.

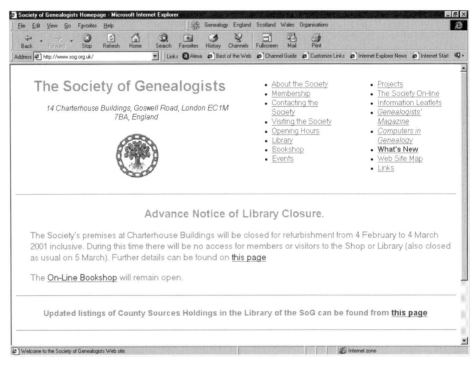

Figure 11.9 The society will close shortly for refurbishment.

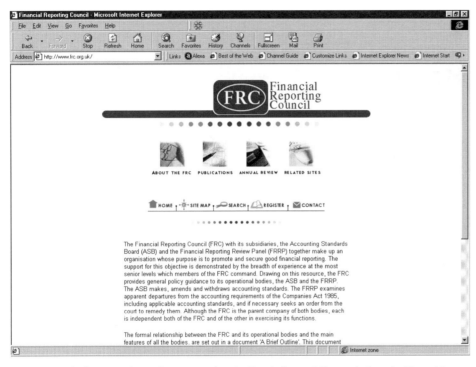

Figure 11.10 Guessing the website name for the Family Record Centre led to the Financial
Reporting Council.

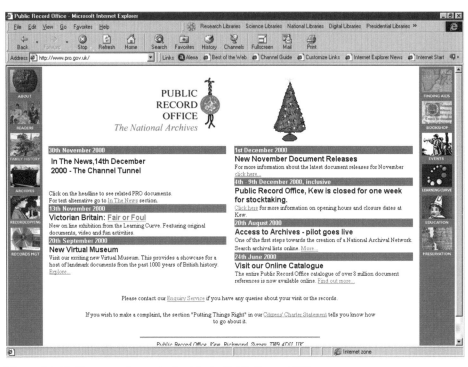

Figure 11.11 There was better luck with the Public Record Office.

If I were to proceed I would make use of each of the sites I visited by digging deeper into them to find information on the family name of Waters. I would continue to record on the worksheet any other sites I visited.

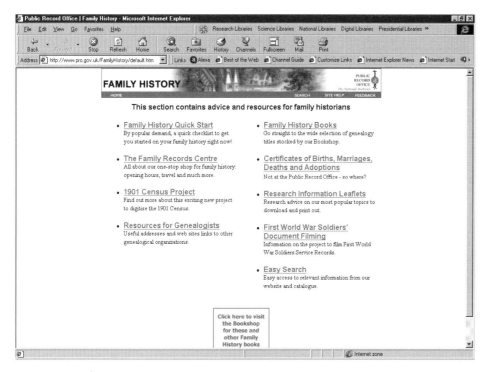

Figure 11.12 Clicking on the Family History graphic allows you to continue your search.

The next step would then be to use the search engine I chose in question 6 of the first section of the worksheet so that I could find more relevant sites to

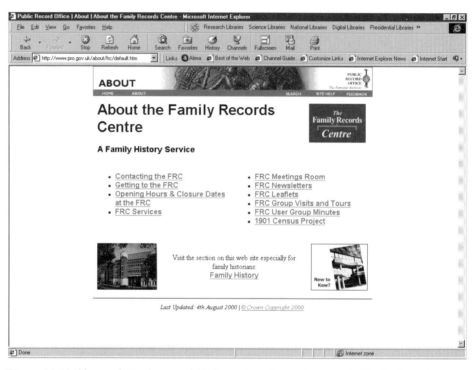

Figure 11.13   Many websites have useful links, such as the one here to the Family Records Centre.

help me. Figure 11.14 shows the home page of the Interactive Web Search Wizard tool. It is a very intuitive tool to use and I described its use earlier in Chapter 3, 'The right tools for the job'.

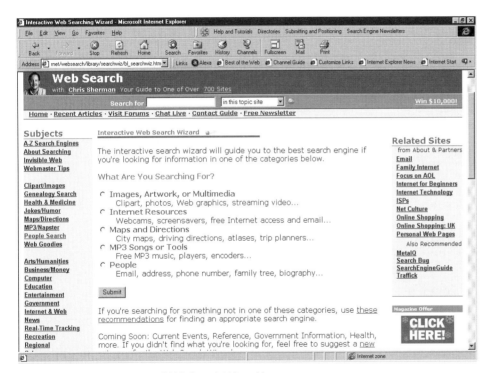

Figure 11.14 The Interactive Web Search Wizard home page.

Finally, I would use a natural language search engine to locate further sources of the name Waters using the questions I phrased on my worksheet. Figure 11.15

shows the results returned by the Ask Jeeves UK site when I enter the question 'Where can I find information about the waters family tree?'.

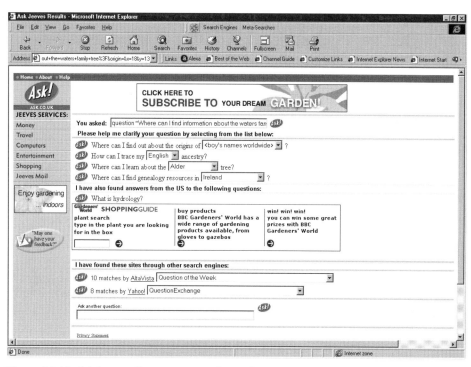

Figure 11.15 Ask Jeeves offers suggestions for tracking down the Waters family tree.

The future of searching 12

What is the future for search technology?

What is the future for search technology?

I would like to end this guide with some of my thoughts on the future of search technology on the internet. Over the past ten years we have seen search engines go from a simple 'look up my search keyword in your database' type of search to 'let me interpret the meaning of your search phrase' to produce more relevant results. We have also seen the advent of specialist software products dedicated to combining the results of searches across many search engines and websites.

The model of tomorrow will do away with the need for a single monolithic search engine. Instead a 'virtual engine' that will perform searches by using many hundreds of co-operative computers, each performing a search of their local database, will satisfy your request. The software running on the researcher's computer will take the results from these many computers and compile them into a categorised list tailored to the meaning of the search phrase.

In fact, we have already seen two examples of just such an engine. Napster, an MP3 music search engine, searched the hard disks of hundreds of computers owned by Napster members to locate music files. Gnutella (which can be found at **http://www.gnutella.com**) uses this same principle to search for all sorts of files.

One of the original developers of Gnutella has gone on to develop InfraSearch (based on the Gnutella engine) which works by using many different computers, each of which has the InfraSearch software installed, to locate any type of information. If you are interested in InfraSearch, take a look at **http://www.gonesilent.com**.

The advantages of these types of 'virtual engines' is that they are infinitely scalable as the searches are performed by multiple computers and each search engine has to search only its own disk drives. Also, they will always access current information because it will be easier to maintain the currency of documents on a single computer, thus doing away with the need for a software spider to have to index millions of web pages, so more of the web can be covered faster.

This technology can only be good news for people like you and I who use the internet every day, and we have only started to scratch the surface of its capabilities. When using the internet for your research it is important to remember the old saying: 'Work smarter, not harder.'

'Surfing' the internet need not be a waste of time as long as you have a clearly defined strategy, know the tools that are at your disposal, know where those tools are to be found, and can use those tools effectively.

Happy searching.

Appendices

Appendix A – internet domain extensions
Appendix B – worksheets

Appendix A

List of internet domain name extensions by country

If you need to work out the URL of a website, it is useful to know the extensions that are used for the various countries around the world.

For example, if you know the company you are looking for is based in Italy, then by looking up this country in the list below you will be able to find its domain name extension which is '.it'. So the complete URL would look something like **www.nameofcompany.it.**

If you come across a website with a domain name extension you do not recognise, you can look it up here also.

Here is the full list of codes. Those countries with an internet domain of '---' do not currently have a domain assigned to them.

Name of area/country/item	Internet domain
Abu Dhabi (UAE)	AE
Academic internet clients	EDU
Adeli Land	---
Afghanistan	---
Ajman (UAE)	AE

Name of area/country/item	Internet domain
Alaska (USA)	AK.US
Albania	AL
Algeria	DZ
American Samoa	AS
America OnLine clients	AOL.COM
Andorra	AD
Angola	AO
Anguilla (BWI)	AI
Antarctica	AQ
Antigua & Barbuda (BWI)	AG
Argentina	AR
Aruba (Neth. Antilles)	AW
Ascension Island	---
Australia	AU
Austria	AT
Azores (Portugal)	---
Bahamas	BS
Bahrain	BH

Name of area/country/item	Internet domain
Balearic Islands (Spain)	---
Bangladesh	BD
Barbados (BWI)	BB
Belgium	BE
Belize (Br. Honduras)	BZ
Benin (Dahomey)	BJ
Bermuda	BM
Bhutan	BT
Bolivia	BO
Bonaire (Neth. Antilles)	---
Bophuthatswana (S.A.)	---
Botswana	BW
Brazil	BR
Brazzaville (Congo/Zaire)	CG
Br. Ind. Ocean Ter. (Chr. Is.)	IO
British Virgin Islands	VG
Brunei Darussalam	BN

Name of area/country/item	Internet domain
Bulgaria	BG
Burkina Faso	BF
Burma	---
Burundi	BI
CIS (Former USSR)	SU
Caicos Islands & Turks	---
Cambodia (Kampuchea)	KH
Cameroon	CM
Canada	CA
Canal Zone (Panama)	PA
Canary Islands (Spain)	---
Cape Verde Islands	CV
Caroline Islands	---
Carriacou Islands (BWI)	---
Cayman Islands (BWI)	KY
Central African Republic	CF
Ceylon (Sri Lanka)	LK

▶

Name of area/country/item	Internet domain
Chad	TD
Chatham Islands (NZ)	---
Chile	CL
China, Peoples Republic	CN
China, Republic of (Taiwan)	TW
Christmas Island (Indian)	IO
Christmas Island (Pacific)	CX
Cocos – Keeling Island	CC
Columbia	CO
Comoros, F & I Republic	KM
Commercial internet clients	COM
Compuserve clients	COMPUSERVE.COM
Congo, Republic of (Zaire)	CG
Cook Islands (Rarotonga)	CK
Corsica (France)	---
Costa Rica	CR
Cote D'Ivoire	CI

Name of area/country/item	Internet domain
Cuba	CU
Curaco (Netherlands Ant.)	---
Cyprus	CY
Czechoslovakia	CS
Dahomey Peoples Republic (Benin)	BJ
Denmark	DK
Diego Garcia Island	---
Djibouti Republic	DJ
Dominica (BWI)	DM
Dominican Republic	DO
Dubai (UAE)	AE
East Timor	TP
Ecuador	EC
Egypt	EG
Ellice Island (Tuvalu)	TV
El Salvador	SV
England (UK)	UK

Name of area/country/item	Internet domain
Equatorial Guinea	GQ
Estonia	EE
Ethiopia	ET
Falkland Islands	FK
Faroe (Faeroe) Islands	FO
Fidonet clients	FIDONET.ORG
Fiji	FJ
Finland	FI
Formosa (Taiwan)	TW
France	FR
French Antilles	---
French Guiana	GF
French Polynesia	PF
French Southern Territory	TF
Fujaira (UAE)	AE
Futuna & Wallis Islands	WF
Gabon Republic	GA

Name of area/country/item	Internet domain
Gambia	GM
German X.400 national network	DBP.DE
Germany	DE
Ghana	GH
Gibraltar	GI
Government internet clients	GOV
Great Britain/Northern Ireland	UK
Greece	GR
Greenland	GL
Grenada (BWI)	GD
Grenadines & St Vincent	VC
Guadeloupe (Fr. Ant.)	GP
Guam	GU
Guantanamo Bay USN	---
Guatemala	GT
Guinea-Bissau	GW
Guinea, Peoples Republic	GN

▶

Name of area/country/item	Internet domain
Guyana	GY
Haiti	HT
Hawaii (USA)	HI.US
Heard and McDonald Islands	HM
Holland (Netherlands)	NL
Honduras, Republic of	HN
Hong Kong	HK
Hungary	HU
Iceland	IS
India	IN
Indonesia	ID
International internet clients	INT
Internet academic clients	EDU
Aviation	AERO (available from June 2001)
Businesses	BIZ (available from June 2001)
Internet commercial clients	COM
Co-operatives	COOP (available from June 2001)

Name of area/country/item	Internet domain
Internet government clients	GOV
Information	INFO (available from June 2001)
Internet international clients	INT
Internet military clients	MIL
Museums	MUSEUM (available from June 2001)
Internet network providers	NET
Personal website	NAME (available from June 2001)
Internet organisational clients	ORG
Professionals	PRO (available from June 2001)
Iran	IR
Iraq	IQ
Ireland, Northern (UK)	UK
Ireland, Republic of (Eire)	IE
Israel	IL
Italy	IT
Ivory Coast	---

Name of area/country/item	Internet domain
Jamaica (BWI)	JM
Japan	JP
Jordan	JO
Kampuchea (Cambodia)	KH
Kenya	KE
Kerguelan Archipelago	---
Kiribati Republic	KI
Korea, North	KP
Korea, Republic of (South)	KR
Kuwait	KW
Laos, Peoples Democratic Republic of	LA
Latvia	LV
Lebanon	LB
Lesotho	LS
Liberia	LR
Libyan Arab Jamahiriya	LY
Liechtenstein	LI

Name of area/country/item	Internet domain
Lithuania	LT
Luxembourg	LU
Macao (Macau)	MO
Madagascar, Democratic Republic	MG
Madeira Island (Portugal)	---
Malawi	MW
Malaysia	MY
Maldives	MV
Mali, Republic of	ML
Malta	MT
Mariana Island (Saipan)	---
Marshall Island	MH
Martinique (French Ant.)	MQ
Mauritania, Islamic Republic	MR
Mauritius	MU
Mayotte (France)	---
Mexico	MX

Name of area/country/item	Internet domain
Micronesia	FM
Midway Island	---
Military internet clients	MIL
Monaco	MC
Mongolian Peoples Republic	MN
Montserrat (BWI)	MS
Morocco	MA
Mozambique	MZ
Myanmar, Union of	MM
Namibia (SW Africa)	NA
Nauru	NR
Nepal	NP
Netherland Antilles	AN
Netherlands (Holland)	NL
Network gateways, internet	NET
Neutral zone	NT
Nevis [St Kitts] (BWI)	KN

Name of area/country/item	Internet domain
New Caledonia	NC
New Guinea, Papua	PG
New Hebrides (Vanuatu)	VU
New Zealand	NZ
Nicaragua	NI
Niger Republic	NE
Nigeria, Federal Republic	NG
Niue Island	NU
Norfolk Island	NF
Northern Cyprus (Turkey)	---
Northern Ireland (UK)	UK
Northern Mariana Island	MP
Norway	NO
Okinawa (Japan)	JP
Oman	OM
Organisational internet clients	ORG
Pakistan	PK

▶

Name of area/country/item	Internet domain
Palau	PW
Panama	PA
Papua New Guinea	PG
Paraguay	PY
Peru	PE
Philippines	PH
Pitcairn Island	PN
Poland	PL
Portugal, Madeira & Azores	PT
Principe, Sao Tome &	ST
Puerto Rico	PR
Qatar	QA
Ras Al Khaymah (UAE)	AE
Reunion Island	RE
Rodriquez Island	---
Romania	RO
Russia (formerly USSR)	SU

Name of area/country/item	Internet domain
Rwanda	RW
Ryukyu Island (Okinawa)	JP
Saba (Neth. Ant.)	---
Saipan (N. Mariana Island)	MP
Samoa, American	AS
Samoa, Western	WS
San Marino	SM
Sao Tome & Principe	ST
Saudi Arabia	SA
Senegal Republic	SN
Seychelles	SC
Sharjah (UAE)	AE
Sierra Leone	SL
Singapore	SG
Slovenia	SI
Solomon Island	SB
Somali	SO

Name of area/country/item	Internet domain
South Africa	ZA
South Georgia	---
Southwest Africa/Namibia	NA
Spain	ES
Spanish North Africa	---
Spitzbergen (Svalbard)	SJ
Sri Lanka (Ceylon)	LK
St Barthelemy (Fr. Ant.)	---
St Christopher (BWI)	---
St Kitts – Nevis (BWI)	KN
St Croix (US VI)	VI
St Eustatius (Neth. Ant.)	---
St Helena	SH
St Lucia (BWI)	LC
St Maarten (Neth. Ant.)	---
St Martin (Fr. Ant.)	---
St Paul & Amsterdam Island	---

Name of area/country/item	Internet domain
St Pierre/Miquelon Island	PM
St Thomas (US VI)	VI
S. Thome Island (PWA)	---
St Vincent/Grenadines (WI)	VC
Sudan	SD
Suriname, Republic of	SR
Svalbard & Jan Mayen Island	SJ
Swaziland	SZ
Sweden	SE
Switzerland	CH
Syrian Arab Republic	SY
Tahiti (French Polynesia)	---
Taiwan (Republic of China)	TW
Tanzania (Zanzibar)	TZ
Thailand	TH
Tibet	---
Timor, East	TP

▶

Name of area/country/item	Internet domain
Togolese Republic	TG
Tokelau Island	TK
Tonga Island	TO
Tortola (Br. VI)	---
Transkei Republic	---
Trinidad & Tobago (BWI)	TT
Tristan Da Cunha	---
Tunisia	TN
Turkey	TR
Turks & Caicos Islands	TC
Tuvalu (Ellice Island)	TV
Uganda	UG
Ukraine	UA
Umm Al Quwain (UAE)	AE
United Arab Emirates	AE
United Kingdom	UK
United States	US

Name of area/country/item	Internet domain
United States – Alabama	AL.US
United States – Alaska	AK.US
United States – Arizona	AZ.US
United States – Arkansas	AZ.US
United States – California	CA.US
United States – Colorado	CO.US
United States – Connecticut	CT.US
United States – Delaware	DE.US
United States – Dist. of Columbia	DC.US
United States – Florida	FL.US
United States – Georgia	GA.US
United States – Idaho	ID.US
United States – Illinois	IL.US
United States – Indiana	IN.US
United States – Iowa	IA.US
United States – Kansas	KS.US
United States – Kentucky	KY.US

▶

Name of area/country/item	Internet domain
United States – Louisiana	LA.US
United States – Maine	ME.US
United States – Maryland	MD.US
United States – Massachusetts	MA.US
United States – Michigan	MI.US
United States – Minnesota	MN.US
United States – Mississippi	MS.US
United States – Missouri	MS.US
United States – Montana	MT.US
United States – Nebraska	NE.US
United States – Nevada	NV.US
United States – New Hampshire	NH.US
United States – New Jersey	NJ.US
United States – New Mexico	NM.US
United States – New York	NY.US
United States – North Carolina	NC.US
United States – North Dakota	ND.US
United States – Ohio	OH.US

Name of area/country/item	Internet domain
United States – Oklahoma	OK.US
United States – Oregon	OR.US
United States – Pennsylvania	PA.US
United States – Rhode Island	RI.US
United States – South Carolina	SC.US
United States – Tennessee	TN.US
United States – Texas	TX.US
United States – Utah	UT.US
United States – Vermont	VT.US
United States – Virginia	VA.US
United States – Washington	WA.US
United States – West Virginia	WV.US
United States – Wisconsin	WI.US
United States – Wyoming	WY.US
Upper Volta	---
Uruguay	UY
USSR [Russia] (CIS)	SU
UUNet clients	UUNET.NET

▶

Name of area/country/item	Internet domain
Vanuatu (New Hebrides)	VU
Vatican City	VA
Venda	---
Venezuela	VE
Vietnam	VN
Virgin Islands, British	VG
Virgin Islands, US	VI
Wake Island	---
Wallis & Futuna Islands	WF
Western Sahara	EH
Western Samoa	WS
Yemen Arab Republic (Formerly N.)	YE
Yemen Democratic Republic (Formerly S.)	YE
Yugoslavia	YU
Zaire	ZR
Zambia	ZM
Zanzibar (Tanzania)	TZ
Zimbabwe (Rhodesia)	ZW

Appendix B

Search strategy worksheet

Use this worksheet to plan your search strategy before you go online. This will maximise the use of your time online and reduce the frustration normally associated with web 'surfing'.

Who or what are you searching for?

1. What type of information do you need (eg statistics, background information, sources, information about a particular person)?

_____

_____

_____

_____

_____

▶

2. What type of resources would be helpful to you (eg reports, articles, government records)?

_____

_____

_____

_____

_____

3. Are there any recognised experts in your subject area you could consult directly online? Do they have a website?

Name of expert	email address	website address

4. What are you trying to do (eg confirm a fact, find new information for the first time, add to your knowledge of a subject, etc)?

_____

_____

_____

_____

_____

5. Is the information you are seeking likely to be available online? If it is confidential, you may not be able to find it.

   Yes, it is online/No, it is not online* (* delete whichever is not applicable)

6. Which search tool is most appropriate for your needs (tick the one you will use)? Refer to Chapters 3 and 4 to help you decide.

   ___ **Interactive Web Search Wizard**
   http://websearch.about.com/internet/websearch/library/searchwiz/bl_searchwiz.htm

   ___ **Smartborg**
   http://www.teleport.com/~lensman/sb/

   ___ **AltaVista**
   http://www.altavista.com and http://www.altavista.co.uk

   ___ **Excite**
   http://www.excite.com and http://www.excite.co.uk

___ Northern Light

http://www.northernlight.com

___ HotBot

http://www.hotbot.com

___ Go

http://www.go.com

___ Google

http://www.google.com

What sources will help you?

1. Could any particular company, association, or specialist organisation hold the information you are looking for? Very often you may need to visit only one site to find what you need, especially if that site is dedicated to your search topic.

   List the names of possible organisations here.

   _____

   _____

   _____

   _____

   _____

2. Before trying the larger directories and search engines try to guess the website address of the company, association or organisation. Start with **www.nameofcompany.com.** If it is a government site, **www.nameofagency.gov** may get you there. If it is a defence establishment, '.mil' will be useful. In other countries you will need to also use '.co.uk' for the UK, '.de' for Germany, etc. See Appendix A for a full list of URL extensions by country and type of domain.

Name of organisation, association, etc	Possible name of website

3. If you have found a site that sort of covers what you want but does not satisfy you totally, check to see who is linking to the site. Go to **http://www.altavista.com** and enter in the search box 'link:nameofsite.com' (or .gov, or .mil, etc). This will give you a list of similar sites you can now visit. Of course, you can use this method to also find out who is linking to them and so on. Another site that is useful for this is LinkPopularity which can be found at **http://www.linkpopularity.com.** This will search multiple search engines for links to the website you have entered.

▶

List the websites you find here and visit them next.

_____

_____

_____

_____

_____

_____

_____

_____

4. If you were not able to guess the name of a suitable site, go to a directory such as Yahoo! **(http://www.yahoo.com)** and browse by your subject category. Visit the sites listed but also make a note of the sub-categories you selected in the space below to get to them. They can be used as keywords in the search engines to find even more sites.

_____

_____

_____

_____

_____

5. If you are looking for product information, use a specialised subject directory instead of a general directory. Visit these:

Yahoo!
http://www.yahoo.com or http://www.yahoo.co.uk

InfoMine – scholarly collection of internet resources
http://lib-www.ucr.edu/main.html

eBlast – Britannica's Internet Guide
http://www.eblast.com

The Internet Sleuth – a good tool to find more subject directories
http://www.isleuth.com

Argus Clearinghouse – strong in pop culture, politics, academic resources and other general subjects
http://www.clearinghouse.com

LookSmart
http://www.looksmart.com

Magellan Internet Guide
http://www.mckinley.com

About.com – covers hundreds of subject areas, very high quality
http://www.about.com

Webcrawler
http://www.webcrawler.com

AlphaSearch – a gateway to the academic resources on the web
http://www.calvin.edu/library/as

Direct Search – a directory of subject directories
http://gwis2.circ.gwu.edu/~gprice/direct.htm

Librarian's Index to the Internet – geared towards academic resources and maintained by professional librarians
http://sunsite.berkeley.edu/internetindex

Open Directory Project
http://www.dmoz.org

6. If you are looking for background information in your subject, use one or more of these meta tools.

All-in-One
http://www.allonesearch.com
All-in-One uses dozens of search tools. A particularly useful feature is the 'Other Interesting Searches' function which provides access to an amazing collection of specialised search engines dedicated to specific topics.

Beaucoup! – access to more than 1200 search engines
http://www.beaucoup.com

Dogpile – one of the most thorough meta tools
http://www.dogpile.com

Inference Find – one of the easiest meta tools to use
http://www.infind.com

The Internet Sleuth
http://www.isleuth.com

ProFusion – can email you on a regular basis when new sites covering your subject area come online
http://www.profusion.com

SavvySearch – good for searching in different languages
http://www.savvysearch.com/search

Ixquick
http://www.ixquick.com

7. Go to Ask Jeeves (**http://www.ask.com** or **http://www.ask.co.uk**), Simpli (**http://www.simpli.com**) or Northern Light (**http://www.northernlight.com**) and enter your search as a question such as 'Where can I find information about genealogy?'. This will return a mixture of websites, subject directories and other resources you can explore.

List the questions you will enter into Ask Jeeves, Simpli or Northern Light here.

_____

_____

_____

_____

_____

_____

_____

_____

_____

List the resources you find here.

_____

_____

_____

_____

_____

_____

8. If you still have not found what you are looking for, enter your search keywords listed above (written down from your directory browsing) in the major search engines. **Do not enter single words** in the search box. You will get too many websites and become overwhelmed. **Instead enter a search phrase**. Try to make your search phrase as narrow as possible. If you do not get any sites returned, broaden your search slightly until you do.

List your possible search phrases here.

_____

_____

_____

_____

_____

_____

9. If you are looking for academic resources such as research papers, or all other avenues have failed, try one or more of these 'invisible web' search tools.

Direct Search

http://gwis2.circ.gwu.edu/~gprice/direct.htm

Lycos

http://dir.lycos.com/Reference/Searchable_Databases/

Infomine

http://infomine.ucr.edu/search.phtml

IntelliSeek

http://www.invisibleweb.com

Additional notes

_____

_____

_____

_____

_____

_____

Evaluating internet resources worksheet

Use this worksheet to evaluate the quality of the resources you find on the internet. This worksheet can be used to evaluate any type of information you may find online.

Name of resource: _____

Website address (URL): _____

Date evaluated: _____

Validity

Validity of a resource depends on how reliable the content is. You need to remember that anyone can publish anything on the internet so something that appears to be credible may not be and must be scrutinised closely before taking it on trust.

Has the information been filtered by a third party? **Yes/No**

Is the information well researched?   **Yes/No**

Is the resource available in a book format or some other medium?   **Yes/No**

List other formats in which the resource is available and the URL where they can be found

_____

_____

_____

_____

_____

_____

Is there any bias?   **Yes/No**

Are there any references to documents used when researching the information?
Yes/No

List any appropriate references here for further investigation

_____

_____

_____

_____

_____

_____

Is there a bibliography?   **Yes/No**

List any appropriate resources here

_____

_____

_____

_____

_____

_____

Accuracy

Accuracy depends on the correctness of the information contained in the resource. The lack of editorial control on the Internet means that resources can range from unintentionally inaccurate to downright deceptive.

Has the information been checked by someone else such as an editor? Yes/No

Can the content be cross-checked with another resource? Yes/No

List where the resources can be found for cross-checking

_____

_____

_____

_____

_____

Is the author motivated to provide accurate information? **Yes/No**

Are there spelling mistakes or other typographical errors? **Yes/No**

Are there any references or a bibliography?   **Yes/No**

Has the information been cross-checked by the author's peers? **Yes/No**

Is there a date on the document? **Yes/No**

Does the content include sweeping generalisations? **Yes/No**

Does the information change rapidly?   **Yes/No**

Is the information one-sided or does it acknowledge opposing views? **Yes/No**

Reasonableness

Reasonableness involves looking at the resource and assessing how fair, objective and consistent it is.

Is the content offering a balanced, reasoned argument or is it slanted towards some view or organisation? **Yes/No**

Is the resource objective or are the views presented linked to the sponsorship of some organisation or association? **Yes/No**

Are there conflicts of interest between the views put forward and the author's background (will the author benefit in some way)?   **Yes/No**

Are wild claims being made or is emotive language being used?   **Yes/No**

Do any arguments discussed within the document contradict themselves? **Yes/No**

Authority

The authority of a resource depends on the expertise and reputation of the source of it. On the internet the source of the information may not be accurately or correctly attributed. In many cases the source is not identified, sometimes deliberately. There are also a lot of sources that are based on personal opinion.

Who is the author? _____

Who has published the resource? _____

Is it the author a well-known publisher, or a knowledgeable webmaster? **Yes/No**

Can a cross-check of the author's authority be made?   **Yes/No**

Write down the address of the resource(s) where the author can be cross-checked

_____

_____

_____

Is the author's email address readily available? **Yes/No**

Write down the author's email address here: _____

Why should I believe this author over another?   _____

What is the author's education, training, and/or experience in a field relevant to the information? _____

Can the author be contacted (has he/she provided email or postal address, phone number)?   **Yes/No**

Write down the author's contact details here: _____

What is the author's reputation or standing among peers?

_____

_____

What is the author's position (job function, title)? _____

Uniqueness

A resource can be considered unique if it contains a large amount of primary information not obtainable from anywhere else. The majority of information on the internet is simply secondary information such as links to other resources which themselves are secondary.

Does the resource contain anything other than a list of links to third-party sites? **Yes/No**

Does the resource contain any primary information? The 'About Us' link will give you a clue as to the amount of primary information the author has provided. **Yes/No**

Completeness

The completeness of a resource means that it is all available online. How often have you visited a website to find that most of its links are inactive and a big sign saying 'under construction' appears on the first page? Would you trust any information on a site in this state?

Are there any dead links or empty pages?   **Yes/No**

Does the information made available have anything missing?   **Yes/No**

If Yes, what is missing to the best of your knowledge?

_____

_____

_____

_____

Is the full text of the information made available or are you looking at an abstract?
Full text/Abstract only

Comprehensiveness

Another important criterion is the comprehensiveness of the information. For example, if you find a resource called 'The Complete Guide to Website Promotion' does it cover **every** aspect of the subject or is there something missing? Maybe it covers only one aspect of website promotion such as search engine submissions.

Does the resource go into sufficient depth or does it leave many points unexplained?

Comprehensive/Not comprehensive

Are there any obvious gaps?   **Yes/No**

If Yes, list the gaps here that you will need to investigate further.

_____

_____

_____

_____

_____

Look at the contents list. Does it cover everything you would expect it to?
Yes/No

If No, what else would you want it to cover?

_____

_____

_____

_____

_____

Are sources cited? If so are they reputable?   **Yes/No**

Is there a hyperlinked bibliography of cited sources?   **Yes/No**

Are external links for additional information included?   **Yes/No**

If there are any quoted statistics, have their sources been cited?   **Yes/No**

If Yes, write down the sources here.

_____

_____

_____

_____

_____

Information and site integrity

Information and site integrity relate to the accuracy of the resource over time and your ability to access it whenever you need to.

When viewing a resource that is time sensitive it is important to make sure that the information is updated when needed. There is no point using a resource that is five years old if it covers a topic such as computers, for example. Technology is changing almost monthly, therefore any sources covering this topic must be no more than a few months old.

Similarly, you do not want websites to suddenly disappear, or for reports to be deleted from a site, so site integrity is also important.

Is the resource being updated regularly?   **Yes/No**

Write down the date it was last updated: _____

Are there any statements on the site about how frequently the information is supposed to be updated? **Yes/No**

Is there any archive information on the site?   **Yes/No**

How frequently are documents moved to the archive area of the site?

_____

Is there a website version number or last updated date?   **Yes/No**

Are all the links on the site still active?   **Yes/No**

Additional notes

_____

_____

_____

_____

_____

Bibliography

Dreyfus, M. A and Young, R. *Simple Guide to The Internet*, Prentice Hall, 2001.

Fouchard, G. A and Young, R. *Simple Guide to Searching the Internet*, Prentice Hall, 2001.

Krol, E. *The Whole Internet*, O'Reilly and Associates, Inc, 1992.

Schlein, A.M. *Find It Online*, Facts on Demand Press, USA, 1999.

Writers' & Artists' Yearbook 1999, A & C Black, 1999.

Websites

About.com **http://www.about.com**

Alexa **http://www.alexa.com**

All-in-One **http://www.allonesearch.com**

AlphaSearch **http://www.calvin.edu/library/as**

AltaVista **http://www.altavista.com** and **http://www.altavista.co.uk**

AnyWho **http://www.anywho.com**

Argus Clearinghouse **http://www.clearinghouse.com**

Ask an Expert **http://www.askanexpert.com.**

Ask Jeeves **http://www.ask.com** and **http://www.ask.co.uk**

Bartlett's Quotations **http://www.cc.columbia.edu/acis/bartleby/bartlett**

Beaucoup! **http://www.beaucoup.com**

BotSpot, The **http://www.botspot.com**

Cartia **http://www.cartia.com**

CIA World Factbook **http://www.cia.gov/cia/publications/factbook/index.html**

CNN News **http://www.cnn.com**

Commonplace Book, The
http://metalab.unc.edu.ibic/CommonplaceBook. html

Copernic **http://www.copernic.com**

DejaNews **http://www.dejanews.com**

Digital Librarian **http://www.digital-librarian.com**

Direct Search **http://gwis2.circ.gwu.edu/~gprice/direct.htm**

Dogpile **http://www.dogpile.com**

eBlast **http://www.eblast.com**

Encyclopedia.Com **http://www.encyclopedia.com**

Excite **http://www.excite.com**

Excite NewsTracker **http://nt.excite.com**

FACSNET **http://facsnet.org/sources_online/main.htm**

FAQ Finder **http://ps.superb.net/FAQ**

ForumOne **http://www.forumone.com**

Free Agent **http://www.forteinc.com**

Free Pint **http://www.freepint.co.uk**

Geocities **http://www.geocities.com/capitolHill/1236/servers.html**

Gnutella **http://www.gnutella.com**

Go **http://www.go.com**

Google **http://www.google.com**

Hotbot **http://www.hotbot.com**

Interactive Websearch Wizard **http://websearch.about.com/internet/ websearch/library/searchwiz/ bl_searchwiz.htm**

Inference Find **http://www.infind.com**

InfoMine **http://lib-www.ucr.edu/main.html**

Informant, The **http://informant.dartmouth.edu**

InfoSpace **http://www.infospace.com**

InfraSearch **http://www.gonesilent.com**

IntelliSeek **http://www.invisibleweb.com**

International White and Yellow Pages **http://www.wayp.com**

Internet Address Finder **http://www.iaf.net**

Internet News Bureau **http://www.newsbureau.com**

Internet Public Library **http://www.ipl.org**

Internet Sleuth, The **http://www.isleuth.com**

Ipswitch **http://www.ipswitch.com**

Ixquick **http://www.ixquick.com**

Librarian's Index to the Internet
http://sunsite.berkeley.edu/internetindex

LinkPopularity **http://www.linkpopularity.com**

Liszt **http://www.liszt.com**

Looksmart **http://www.looksmart.com**

Lycos **http://dir.lycos.com/Reference/Searchable_Databases/**

Magellan Internet Guide **http://www.mckinley.com**

MetaCrawler **http://www.metacrawler.com**

Meta-Email-Search-Agent **http://mesa.rrzn.uni-hannover.de**

Mind-it **http://www.netmind.com/html/url-minder.html**

Moreover.com **http://www.moreover.com**

Nedsite **http://www.nedsite.nl/search/people.htm**

NET-HAPPENINGS
http://listserv.classroom.com/archives/net-happenings.html

NewsBytes **http://www.newsbytes.com**

NewsHub **http://www.newshub.com**

NewsNow **http://www.newsnow.co.uk**

Northern Light **http://www.northernlight.com**

Northern Light News Page **http://www.northernlight.com/news/**

Open Directory Project **http://www.dmoz.org**

Pandia Search Central **http://www.pandia.com**

PR Newswire **http://www.prnewswire.com**

PR Web **http://www.prweb.com**

ProfNet **http://www.profnet.com**

ProFusion **http://www.profusion.com**

ResearchBuzz **http://www.researchbuzz.com**

Research-it! **http://www.itools.com/research-it**

SavvySearch **http://www.savvysearch.com/search**

Search Engines **http://www.searchengines.com**

Search Engine Showdown **http://www.searchengineshowdown.com**

Search Engine Watch **http://www.searchenginewatch.com**

Search Engine World **http://www.searchengineworld.com**

SearchIQ **http://www.searchiq.com**

SearchProcess **http://www.searchprocess.com/eng/**

Simpli **http://www.simpli.com**

Smartborg **http://www.teleport.com/~lensman/sb/**

Sources & Experts **http://metalab.unc.edu/slanews/internet/experts.html**

Spyonit **http://www.spyonit.com**

StuffIt **http://www.aladdinsys.com/stuffit/**

Switchboard **http://www.switchboard.com**

TheBrain **http://www.thebrain.com**

TracerLock **http://www.peacefire.org/tracerlock/**

Tucows **http://www.tucows.com**

UCmore **http://www.ucmore.com**

Ultimate White Pages **http://www.theultimates.com/white**

Usenet FAQs **http://www.faqs.org/usenet**

Virtual Reference Desk
http://thohrplus.lib.purdue.edu/reference/index html

Webcrawler **http://www.webcrawler.com**

WebSearch **http://websearch.about.com**

WebWire **http://www.webwire.com**

Whatsnu **http://www.whatsnu.com**

WhoWhere? **http://www.whowhere.com**

WinZip **http://www.winzip.com**

World Email Directory **http://www.worldemail.com**

WorldPages Global Find **http://www.worldpages.com/global**

Yahoo! **http://www.yahoo.com** and **http://www.yahoo.co.uk**

Yahoo! News Coverage **http://headlines.yahoo.com/Full_Coverage/**

Yahoo! People Search (UK) **http://ukie.people.yahoo.com**

Yahoo! People Search (US) **http://people.yahoo.com**

Yahoo! Reference: Quotations **http://www.yahoo.com/reference/quotations**

Zapper **http://www.zapper.com**

Index